**BASIC/NOT BORING
MATH SKILLS**

FOURTH GRADE BOOK OF MATH TESTS

Series Concept & Development
by Imogene Forte & Marjorie Frank

Illustrations by Kathleen Bullock

Incentive Publications, Inc.
Nashville, Tennessee

About the cover:
Bound resist, or tie dye, is the most ancient known
method of fabric surface design. The brilliance of the
basic tie dye design on this cover reflects the possibilities
that emerge from the mastery of basic skills.

Illustrated by Kathleen Bullock
Cover art by Mary Patricia Deprez, dba Tye Dye Mary®
Cover design by Marta Drayton and Joe Shibley
Edited by Angela Reiner

ISBN 0-86530-463-7

PRINTED IN THE UNITED STATES OF AMERICA
www.incentivepublications.com

TABLE OF CONTENTS

INSIDE THE
FOURTH GRADE BOOK OF MATH TESTS

"I wish I had a convenient, fast way to assess basic skills and standards."
"If only I had a way to find out what my students already know about math!"
"If only I had a good way to find out what my students have learned!"
"How can I tell if my students are ready for state assessments?"
"It takes too long to create my own tests on the units I teach."
"The tests that come with my textbooks are too long and dull."
"I need tests that cover all the skills on a topic—not just a few here and there."

This is what teachers tell us about their needs for testing materials. If you, too, are looking for quality, convenient materials that will help you gauge how well students are moving towards mastering basic skills and standards—look no further. This is a book of tests such as you've never seen before! It's everything you've wanted in a group of ready-made math assessments for fourth graders.

- The tests are student-friendly. One glance through the book and you will see why. Students will be surprised that it's a test at all! The pages are inviting and fun. A clever cat and his many rat friends tumble over the pages, leading students through language questions and problems. Your students will not groan when you pass out these tests. They'll want to stick with them all the way to the end to see which character is holding the STOP sign this time!

- The tests are serious. Do not be fooled by the catchy characters and visual appeal! These are serious, thorough assessments of basic content. As a part of the BASIC/Not Boring Skills Series, they give broad coverage of skills with a flair that makes them favorites of teachers and kids.

- The tests cover all the basic skill areas for math. There are 20 tests within four areas: numbers & computation, problem solving, geometry & measurement, and graphing, statistics, & probability.

- The tests are ready to use. In a convenient and manageable size, each test covers a skill area (such as Problem-Solving strategies, plane geometry, or decimals) that should be assessed. Use the pages for an individual student, or make copies for an entire class. Answer keys (included in back) are easy to find and easy to use.

- Skills are clearly identified. You can see exactly which skills are tested by reviewing the list of skills provided with each group of tests.

HOW TO USE THE
FOURTH GRADE BOOK OF MATH TESTS

Each test can be used in many different ways. Here are a few:

- as a pre-test to see what a student knows or can do on a certain math topic
- as a post-test to find out how well students have mastered a content or skill area
- as a review to check up on student mastery of standards or readiness for state assessments
- as a survey to provide direction for your present or future instruction
- as an instructional tool to guide students through a review of a lesson
- with one student in an assessment or tutorial setting
- with a small group of students for assessment or instruction
- with a whole class for end-of-unit assessment

The Fourth Grade Book of Math Tests provides you with tools for using the tests effectively and keeping track of how students are progressing on skills or standards:

- 20 Tests on the Topics You Need: These are grouped according to broad topics within math. Each large grouping has three or more sub-tests. Tests are clearly labeled with subject area and specific topic.

- Skills Checklists Correlated to Test Items: At the beginning of each group of tests, you'll find a list of the skills covered. (For instance, pages 10–13 hold lists of skills for the eight tests on numbers and computation.) Each skill is matched with the exact test items assessing that skill. If a student misses an item on the test, you'll know exactly which skill needs sharpening.

- Student Progress Records: Page 122 holds a reproducible form that can be used to track individual student achievement on all the tests in this book. Make a copy of this form for each student, and record the student's test scores and areas of instructional need.

- Class Progress Records: Pages 123–124 hold reproducible forms for keeping track of a whole class. You can record the dates that tests are given, and keep comments about what you learned from that test as well as notes for further instructional needs.

- Reference for Skill-Sharpening Activities: Pages 125–126 describe a program of appealing exercises designed to teach, strengthen, and reinforce basic math skills and content. The skills covered in these books are correlated to national curriculum standards and the standards for many states.

- Scoring Guide for Performance Test: A performance test is given for math problem solving. For a complete scoring guide that assesses student performance on this test, see page 137.

- Answer Keys: An easy-to-use answer key is provided for each of the 16 tests. (See pages 128–143.)

THE 4TH GRADE MATH TESTS

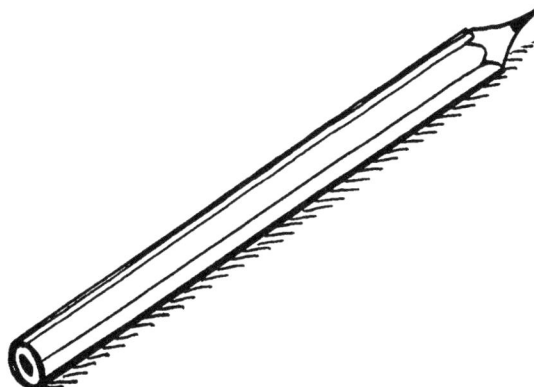

Numbers and Computation Skills Checklists

Numbers & Computation Test # 1:

WHOLE NUMBER CONCEPTS

Test Location: pages 14–19

Skill	*Test Items*
Read and write whole numbers	1–8
Compare and order whole numbers	9–14
Write numbers in expanded notation to show place value	15–17
Identify place value of whole numbers	15–22
Recognize prime numbers	23
Round whole numbers	24–27
Recognize a number in a variety of equivalent forms	28
Identify factors and common factors	29–33
Analyze and extend patterns and sequences	34–38
Estimate numbers and amounts	39–45

Numbers & Computation Test # 2:

ADDITION AND SUBTRACTION

Test Location: pages 20–25

Skill	*Test Items*
Demonstrate knowledge of addition and subtraction facts	1–20
Compute with addition; solve addition problems with 1 to 3-digit addends	21–23, 27, 29, 32
Compute with addition; solve addition problems with addends that are longer than 3-digit addends	24–26
Solve word problems with addition	25, 27, 29
Solve column addition problems	23, 28, 29
Check accuracy of addition and subtraction solutions	30, 31, 37
Compute with subtraction; solve subtraction problems with 1 to 3-digit addends	33, 38
Compute with subtraction; solve subtraction problems with addends that are longer than 3 digits	34, 35, 36
Solve word problems with subtraction	33, 34, 38, 42, 43
Solve addition and subtraction problems with multiples of 10	31, 32, 39–41
Estimate answers to addition and subtraction problems	44–46
Solve equations with addition and subtraction	47–50

Fourth Grade Book of Math Tests

Numbers & Computation Test # 3:

MULTIPLICATION

Test Location: pages 26–29

Skill	*Test Items*
Demonstrate knowledge of multiplication facts	1–20
Compute; solve multiplication problems with 1–digit multiplier	21, 22, 24, 38
Solve word problems with multiplication	21–23, 27, 28, 29
Compute; solve multiplication problems with 2–digit multiplier	23, 25, 26, 27, 29, 34, 39, 40
Check accuracy of (or verify solutions to) multiplication problems	25, 28, 34
Compute; solve multiplication problems with 3 (or more)-digit multiplier	28, 32
Solve multiplication problems with multiples of 10	30, 31, 33, 35, 37
Solve equations using multiplication	35–37
Estimate answers to multiplication problems	38–40

Numbers & Computation Test # 4:

DIVISION

Test Location: pages 30–33

Skill	*Test Items*
Demonstrate knowledge of division facts	1–20
Compute; Solve division problems with 1–digit divisors	21–29, 37
Compute; solve division problems with 2–digit divisors	30–36, 38–40
Solve division problems with multiples of 10	31, 36
Verify answers to (or check accuracy of solutions to) division problems	31, 35
Estimate answers to division problems	38–40
Solve word problems with division	21–23, 28, 29, 32, 33, 38–40
Solve equations with division	31, 36–37

Numbers & Computation Test # 5:

ALL OPERATIONS

Test Location: pages 34–37

Skill	*Test Items*
Choose the correct operation to solve word problems	1–4
Choose the correct operation for equations	5–11
Identify correct order of operations to solve a problem	12–13
Solve a variety of problems using various operations	1, 18–22
Solve equations using a variety of operations	14–17, 24–27
Estimate the answers to problems using various operations	28–30

Numbers & Computation Test # 6:

FRACTIONS

Test Location: pages 38–43

Skill	*Test Items*
Name fractional parts of a whole or set	1–6, 25–27
Read and write fractions and mixed numerals	7–11
Read and write fractions and mixed numerals in words	12–16
Compare and order fractions	17–23
Identify and write fractions in lowest terms	24, 30–32
Identify and write equivalent fractions	28, 29
Write fractions as mixed numerals and mixed numerals as fractions	33–37
Add and subtract fractions with like denominators	38–39
Add and subtract fractions with unlike denominators	40–43
Multiply fractions	44–45
Divide fractions	46–47
Solve equations with fractions	44–45
Solve word problems with fractions	20–23, 28, 29, 36, 37, 42, 48–50
Verify answers or check accuracy of problems	42, 44, 45, 47

DECIMALS

Test Location: pages 44–47

Skill	Test Items
Read and write decimal numerals	1–10
Identify place value in decimals	11–15
Compare and order decimals	16–17
Round decimals	18–20
Multiply and divide decimals	21
Add and subtract decimals	22–23, 35–36
Recognize equivalencies between fractions and decimals	24–32
Recognize percents that are equivalent to fractions	33
Recognize percents that are equivalent to decimals	34, 37
Estimate answers to problems with decimals	38–40
Solve word problems with decimals	38–40

Numbers & Computation Test # 8:

ALGEBRA CONCEPTS

Test Location: pages 48–51

Skill	Test Items
Compare and order integers	1
Use symbols or words to describe the relationship between numbers	2–10
Write or choose an expression to represent a statement; identify meanings of expressions	11–16
Simplify mathematical expressions	16
Choose or write equations to represent problems	17–20
Use equations to solve word problems	18–20, 25–30
Solve equations with whole numbers	26–29
Identify operations to be used in equations	25, 28
Choose the correct equation and use it to solve a problem	20, 27, 30

Fourth Grade Book of Math Tests

WHOLE NUMBER CONCEPTS

Name _____ Possible Correct Answers: 45

Date _____ Your Correct Answers: _____

1. What is the number on banner # 1?
   A. eight hundred fifteen thousand, ten
   B. eighty-five thousand, one hundred
   C. eighty-five thousand, ten
   D. eight thousand, five hundred, one hundred

85,100   1.

2. What is the number on banner # 2?
   A. Two million, two hundred twenty-two
   B. Two hundred twenty-two thousand, two
   C. Two hundred twenty thousand, two hundred two
   D. Two million, two hundred twenty thousand, two hundred two

220, 202 2.

3. Write this numeral in words.
   6,550

   _____

   _____

4. Write this numeral in words.
   12,200

   _____

   _____

5. Write the numeral. _____

   seventy-five thousand, forty

6. Write the numeral. _____

   one hundred twenty-five thousand

7. Write the numeral. _____

   thirty-one thousand, one hundred

8. Write the numeral. _____

   four million

— 14 —

Here are the distances the rats ran in the big rat race.

Rufus	1500 meters
Georgianna	1450 meters
Reggie	1942 meters
Elmo	1589 meters
Jeranamo	1598 meters
Abigail	1455 meters

9. Who ran the greatest distance?

_____

10. Who ran the shortest distance?

_____

11. Circle the greatest number.

5,204 5,042 5,240 5,420

12. Circle the least number.

101,110 110,111 111,111

13. Write these in order from smallest to largest.

6,505   6,517   6,479

_____ _____ _____

14. Write the numbers from Elmo's program in order from smallest to largest.

A. _____

B. _____

C. _____

D. _____

E. _____

F. _____

Al   5,972 points
Val   6,493 points
Mel   6,430 points
Sal   5,903 points
Hal   6,440 points
Wally 6,439 points

15. Which is the correct expanded notation for this number?

29,406

A. 2000 + 900 + 40 + 6

B. 20,000 + 9000 + 400 + 60

C. 20,000 + 9000 + 400 + 6

D. 2000 + 9000 + 400 + 10 + 6

16. Write this number in **expanded notation**.

7,243

_____

17. Write this number in **expanded notation**.

8,498

_____

Fourth Grade Book of Math Tests

18. Circle the numeral in the **tens** place.

578,623

19. Circle the numeral in the **ten thousands** place.

987,654

20. What is the place value of the **3** in this number? **29,385**

_____

21. What is the place value of the **6** in this number? **560,101**

_____

22. Write a numeral with **5** in the **millions** place.

_____

23. Circle the **prime numbers** on the trophy below.

24. Round this number to the nearest **ten**: 3,869

_____

25. Round this number to the nearest **hundred**: 64,215

_____

26. Round this number to the nearest **thousand**:

18,760

_____

27. Round this number to the nearest **ten thousand**:

18,760

_____

Fourth Grade Book of Math Tests

28. All of the flags except one show a number amount that is the same. Circle the flag showing a different amount.

1. *four hundred forty-four*

2. 400 + 40 + 4

3. 4000 + 400 + 4

4. four hundreds four tens four ones

5. **444**

6. 400
   40
   + 4
   _____

---

29. Write all the factors of **15**.	30. Write all the factors of **24**.

---

31. Which numbers on this track are NOT factors of **28**?
Cross them out with an **X**.

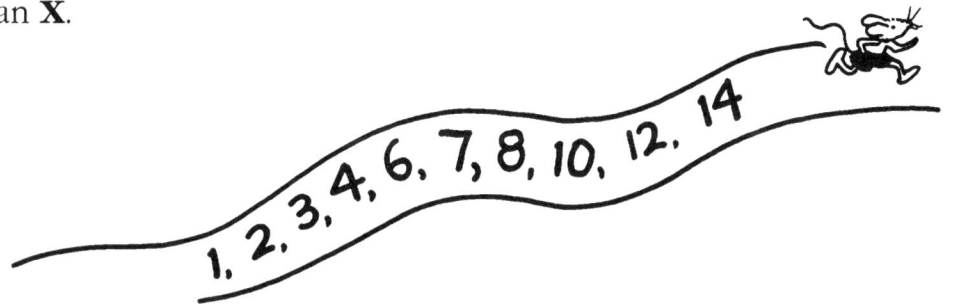

1, 2, 3, 4, 6, 7, 8, 10, 12, 14

32. Which factors on the track are NOT factors of **30**?
Cross them out with an **X**.

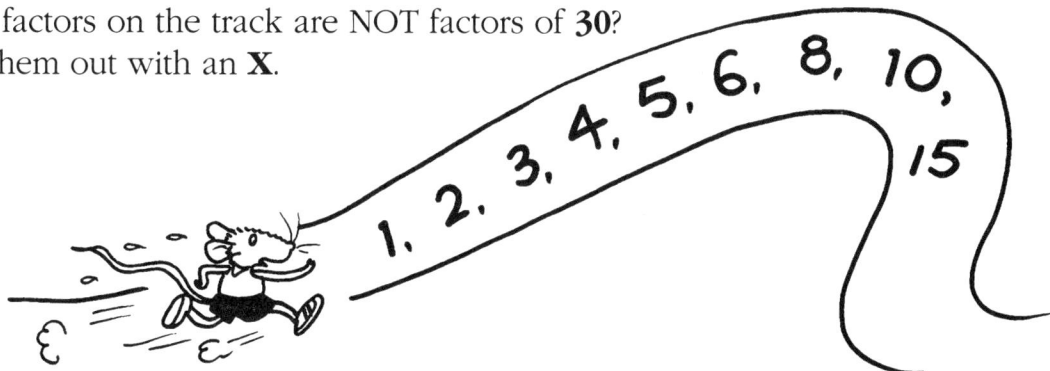

1, 2, 3, 4, 5, 6, 8, 10, 15

Name _____

17

Fourth Grade Book of Math Tests

33. What are the factors that **30** and **15** have in common? Write them in the box.

34. Write the missing number in the box.

   6,   12,   18,   [ ],   30,   36,   42

35. Write the missing numbers in the boxes.

   11,   12,   14,   17,   [ ],   26,   32,   [ ]

36. What comes next? Finish the pattern by writing the correct numbers on the last hurdle.

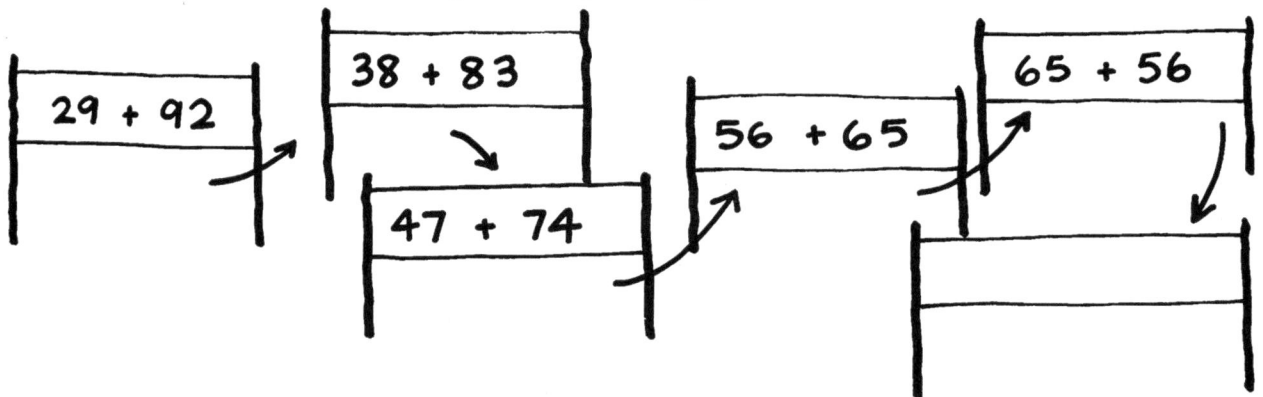

37. Write the missing numbers to finish the pattern.

   500,   450,   400,   350,   [ ], [ ], [ ]

38. Finish the pattern on Georgia's flags.

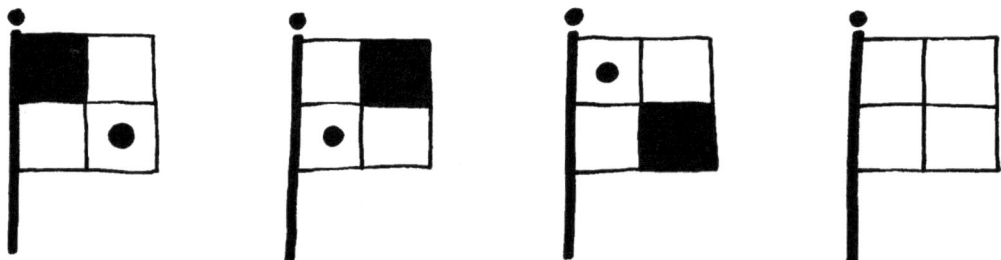

Team Points in State Track Meet

TEAM	POINTS
Comets	3907
Chargers	4605
Hurricanes	4539
Cyclones	4599
Racers	3766
Dashers	4135
Speedsters	3900
Speed Kings	4400

39. Which team has about 4500 points?

_____

40. Which team has about 200 points less than the Chargers?

_____

41. Which number is closest to four hundred thousand? *(Circle one answer.)*

   A. 449,209   C. 391,999

   B. 380,902   D. 460,543

42. Which number is about half of 660,000? *(Circle one answer.)*

   A. 329,888   C. 360,500

   B. 399,222   D. 300,000

Compare the prices of the pole-vaulting poles.

Pole Prices
Gigi's $120
Georgia's $175
Rhoda's $130
Rozzy's $160
Nellie's $280
Fannie's $200
Ellie's $235

43. Whose pole cost more than twice as much as Gigi's pole?

_____

44. Whose pole cost about $100 more than Rhoda's pole?

_____

45. Which shirt has a number that is about 20 more than three other shirts? _____

281   151   130   106   129   132

STOP

Name _____ **19**

ADDITION & SUBTRACTION

Name _____   Possible Correct Answers: 50

Date _____   Your Correct Answers: _____

Caspian has just finished a math test. How did he do?
Check his answers. Circle the number of each problem that he has worked **correctly.**

1. Which is NOT correct?
   a. **6 + 7 = 13**   (c.) **12 + 13 = 26**
   b. **19 – 8 = 11**   d. **8 + 9 = 17**

2. Fill in the box.   **28 –** $\boxed{14}$ **= 14**

3. Fill in the box.   **11 + 11 =** $\boxed{22}$

4. Fill in the box. $\boxed{8}$ **= 15 – 6**

5. Fill in the box.   **17 – 9 =** $\boxed{9}$

6. Fill in the box. $\boxed{13}$ **+ 12 = 25**

7. Fill in the box.   **19 –** $\boxed{12}$ **= 7**

8. Fill in the box.   **16 – 7 =** $\boxed{12}$

9. Fill in the box.   **9 + 9 =** $\boxed{18}$

10. Fill in the box.   **11 –** $\boxed{3}$ **= 7**

11. Fill in the box. $\boxed{4}$ **+ 7 = 12**

12. Fill in the box. $\boxed{1}$ **– 10 = 11**

13. Fill in the box.   **7 +** $\boxed{8}$ **= 15**

14. Which answer is NOT correct?
    a. **11 + 7 = 18**   c. **22 – 9 = 13**
    (b.) **15 – 8 = 8**   d. **20 – 7 = 13**

15. Fill in the box.   **15 +** $\boxed{6}$ **= 21**

16. Fill in the box. $\boxed{11}$ **– 5 = 14**

17. Fill in the box.   **9 +** $\boxed{15}$ **= 24**

18. Which is NOT correct?
    (a.) **9 + 3 = 11**   b. **6 + 8 = 14**

19. Fill in the box.   **9 +** $\boxed{4}$ **= 13**

20. Which is correct?
    a. **13 + 14 = 26**   (b.) **27 – 15 = 12**

Use this chart to solve problems 21–23.

Team Wins over 20 years

Team	Number of Wins
The Tempests	216
The Water Rats	184
The Speed Demons	329
The Comets	88
The Torpedoes	109

21. What is the total number of wins for the two highest-winning teams?

    Answer: _____

22. What is the total number of wins for the two lowest-winning teams?

    Answer: _____

23. What was the total number of wins for all teams?

    Answer: _____

24. Which answer is correct?

$$4,693$$
$$+\ 8,216$$

   A. 13,807   C. 13,909

   B. 12,809   D. 12,909

25. A chain of sporting goods stores sold **28,418** swimsuits to high school swim teams in one year. The next year, they sold **64,382** suits. How many suits did they sell in the two-year period? *(Circle the correct answer.)*

   A. 92,890   C. 92,790

   B. 92,800   D. 82,800

26. Compute:

$$70,398$$
$$+\ 45,665$$

Name _____

Fourth Grade Book of Math Tests

27. A diver won a gold medal in a number of competitions. The number of her wins was the sum of **35** and **18**. How many medals did she win?

Answer: _____

28. Compute.

6,200
470
710
+ 220

30. Rufus is adding up the number of hours he has spent practicing in the past five months.

Has Rufus found the right answer?

(Circle yes or no.)

yes   **no**

140
220
160
210
+ 180
_____
910

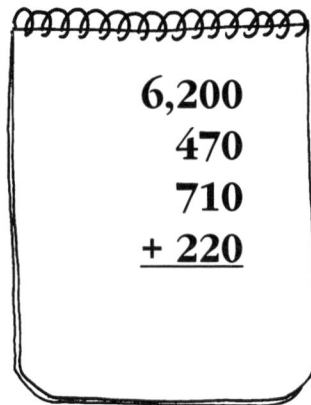

29. During a week of tiring practices, the dive team members drank plenty of fresh water. Figure out how many cups of water were guzzled by these six team members.

Rufus   35 cups
Elmo   42 cups
Sol   19 cups
Reggie   27 cups
Alfredo 36 cups
Felix   29 cups

31. Which problems are solved correctly? *(Circle the letters.)*

A.   **520 + 140 = 660**

B.   **9100 + 610 = 9700**

C.   **800 + 200 + 40 + 50 = 1000**

D.   **550 + 50 + 30 = 580**

E.   **270 + 400 + 20 = 690**

32. Elmo usually lands dives in good form. However, sometimes the dives are terrible flops. In one week, Elmo landed **30** belly flops. The next week he landed **87**! How many flops did Elmo have all together?

Answer: _____

Answer: _____

Name _____

Fourth Grade Book of Math Tests

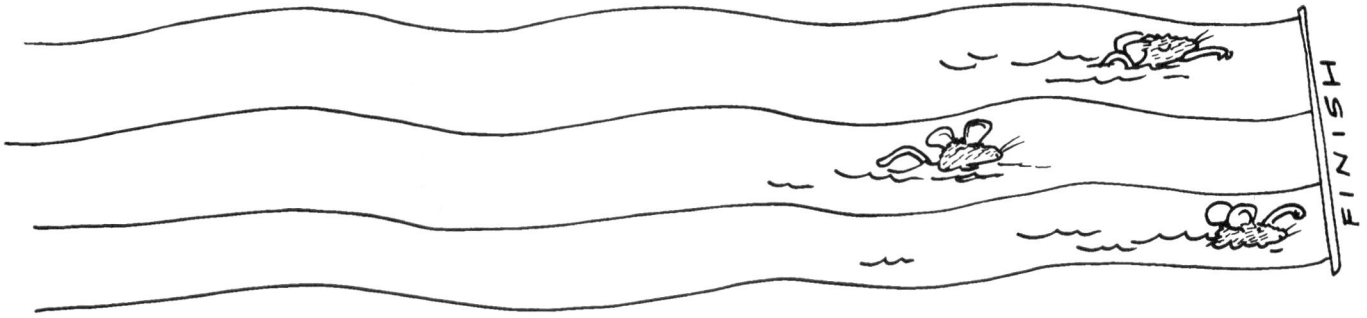

33. Georgio swam 10 laps of the pool in 2800 seconds. Angelo swam 10 laps in 436 seconds less than Georgio. How long did it take Angelo?

Answer: _____

34. A swimmer's age is a number that, when added to **1,981**, gives a sum of **2,000**. What is the swimmer's age?

Answer: _____

36. Compute:

$$58,216 \\ -47,123$$

35. Which answer is correct?

$$773,222 \\ - \ 74,202$$

   A. 701,020

   B. 709,020

   C. 699,020

   D. 847,424

37. Which problems are NOT solved correctly? *(Circle the letters.)*

   A. 95 – 42 = 53

   B. 79 – 33 = 36

   C. 68 – 9 = 57

   D. 57 – 25 = 32

Name _____

Fourth Grade Book of Math Tests

38. There were **500** clean, dry towels at the pool at the beginning of the week. By Friday, **333** towels had been used. How many towels were clean and dry at the end of the week?

Answer: _____

39. Which problems are solved correctly? *(Circle the letters.)*

  A. 2300 + 100 = 2400

  B. 160 + 20 = 190

  C. 400 + 200 + 90 = 429

40. Which problems are solved correctly? *(Circle the letters.)*

  A. 750 − 40 = 705

  B. 1200 − 500 = 700

  C. 820 − 620 = 220

41. Which problems are solved correctly? *(Circle the letters.)*

  A. 780 + 100 − 40 = 800

  B. 70 − 50 + 600 = 620

  C. 50 + 40 − 20 = 70

42. Two teams met for a swimming race. The **Torpedoes** traveled **104** miles to the race. The **Blue Streaks** traveled **67** miles less than the Torpedoes. How far did the Blue Streaks travel?

Answer: _____

43. Last year, the diving team spent **$2875** on medical bills for diving injuries. This year, the team spent **$1200** more. How much did the team spend this year?

Answer: _____

Name _____

24

Use this chart for questions 44–46.

Swimming Practice

Week	Hours of Practice
Week #1	34
Week # 2	42
Week # 3	29
Week # 4	
Week # 5	13
Week # 6	20
Total	159

44. The total hours for six weeks is shown on the chart. The hours for week # 4 is missing. About how many hours were practiced in week 4?
    A. about 10 hours
    B. about 40 hours
    C. about 20 hours
    D. about 50 hours

45. About how many hours did the team practice in the first three weeks?
    A. about 100
    B. about 130
    C. about 120
    D. about 80

46. About how many more hours were practiced in the first two weeks than in the last two weeks?
    A. about 40
    B. about 20
    C. about 10
    D. about 30

Find the missing numbers in the equations below.

47. $94 - 30 + x = 70$

    $x =$ [ ]

48. $500 + n = 540$

    $n =$ [ ]

49. $x - 250 = 0$

    $x =$ [ ]

50. $3000 - n = 1999$

    $n =$ [ ]

Fourth Grade Book of Math Tests

MULTIPLICATION

Name _____   Possible Correct Answers: 40

Date _____   Your Correct Answers: _____

Georgia has just finished a math test. How did she do?
Check her answers.
Circle the number of each problem that she has correctly answered.

1. Which is NOT correct?

   a. **5 x 6 = 30**   c. **8 x 4 = 32**

   (b) **3 x 8 = 28**   d. **6 x 4 = 24**

2. Fill in the box.   **7 x** ⟨7⟩ **= 49**

3. Fill in the box.   **11 x 4 =** ⟨44⟩

4. Fill in the box. ⟨64⟩ **= 8 x 9**

5. Fill in the box.   **6 x 7 =** ⟨49⟩

6. Fill in the box. ⟨9⟩ **x 4 = 36**

7. Fill in the box.   **5 x** ⟨11⟩ **= 55**

8. Fill in the box.   **9 x 6 =** ⟨54⟩

9. Fill in the box.   **8 x 7 =** ⟨54⟩

10. Fill in the box.   **6 x** ⟨6⟩ **= 36**

11. Fill in the box. ⟨9⟩ **x 8 = 72**

12. Fill in the box. ⟨12⟩ **x 2 = 24**

13. Fill in the box. **7 x** ⟨4⟩ **= 35**

14. Which answer is NOT correct?

   a. **10 x 8 = 80** (c.) **9 x 5 = 40**

   b. **3 x 9 = 27**   d. **4 x 7 = 28**

15. Fill in the box. **6 x** ⟨8⟩ **= 48**

16. Fill in the box. ⟨7⟩ **x 7 = 63**

17. Fill in the box. **8 x** ⟨8⟩ **= 64**

18. Which is NOT correct?

   a. **12 x 3 = 36**   (b.) **4 x 13 = 42**

19. Fill in the box. **9 x** ⟨9⟩ **= 81**

20. Which is correct?

   (a.) **2 x 3 x 3 = 18**   b. **5 x 4 x 2 = 11**

Use this chart for problems 21–23.

What We Saw Underwater

Diver	Number of Fish	Number of Lobsters
Elmo	133	2
Georgia		4
Reggie	266	0
Alberto	179	1
Rufus		3
Alfonso	84	3

21. Georgia saw **16** times as many fish as lobsters. How many fish did she see?

    Answer: _____

22. Rufus saw **50** times as many fish as lobsters. How many fish did he see?

    Answer: _____

23. Felix went on a diving trip. He saw **14** times as many fish as Alfonso saw on his trip the day before. (See the chart.) How many fish did Felix see?

    Answer: _____

24. Compute:

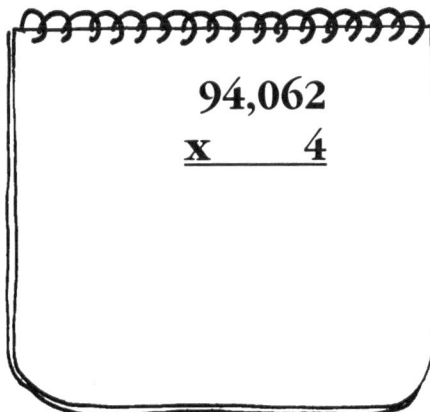

$$
\begin{array}{r}
94{,}062 \\
\times \quad 4 \\
\hline
\end{array}
$$

25. Is this answer correct?
    (Circle yes or no.)

$$
\begin{array}{r}
49 \\
\times\, 25 \\
\hline
1225
\end{array}
$$

    yes   no

26. What is the missing number?

    4   16   64   [   ]   1024

27. If divers saw **39** sharks in a month, how many did they see in a year if this rate stayed the same?

    Answer: _____

Fourth Grade Book of Math Tests

28. Elmo has joined an *Underwater Adventures* Dive Trip.
He has heard that this company took 215 divers on trips
last week. Each diver pays $180 for a trip.
Elmo calculated the total cost for these divers.
Did he get the correct answer? *(Circle yes or no.)*

$$\begin{array}{r} \$\,180 \\ \times\,215 \\ \hline \$\,37{,}300 \end{array}$$

yes   no

29. The cook for the dive trip packs dry food ahead of time. He is packing **37** meals for each diver for the ten-day trip. There are **96** divers going out on trips. How many meals will he need to pack?

Answer: _____

30. Circle the problems that have correct answers.

A. **30 x 6 = 180**

B. **7 x 200 = 140**

C. **40 x 80 = 320**

D. **50 x 700 = 35,000**

E. **9 x 800 = 7,200**

F. **300 x 20 = 6,000**

31. What is the missing number?
(Circle the correct answer.)

60 x _____ = 4200

A. 7   C. 70

B. 700   D. 7000

32. Compute:

$$\begin{array}{r} 622 \\ \times\,514 \\ \hline \end{array}$$

33. Which factor is missing from this division problem?
(Circle the correct answer.)

54,000 ÷ _____ = 60

A. 900   C. 9

B. 90   D. 9000

Name

Fourth Grade Book of Math Tests

Copyright ©2000 by Incentive Publications, Inc., Nashville, TN.

34. Show that Caspian's answer is correct.

$$19,321$$
$$\times \quad 55$$
$$1,062,655$$

35. Solve this problem to find **x**.

$$x = 90 \times 40$$

$$x = \boxed{}$$

36. Solve this problem to find **n**.

$$122 \times n = 244$$

$$n = \boxed{}$$

37. Solve this problem to find **y**.

$$800 \times y = 4,800$$

$$y = \boxed{}$$

38. A company makes **485** life preservers a month. Estimate the number they would make in **9** months.

Your estimate: _____

39. Some divers go shopping for wet suits. There are **42** divers. The suits cost **$292** each. Estimate the total cost of the suits.

Your estimate: _____

40. Alfonso counted **37** schools of fish today. Each school had about **200** fish in it. Estimate the number of fish Alfonso saw.

Your estimate: _____

Name _____

29

DIVISION

Name _____   Possible Correct Answers: 40

Date _____   Your Correct Answers: _____

Elmo has just finished a math test. How did he do? Check his answers.
Circle the number of each problem that he has done correctly.

1. Which is NOT correct?
   - a. $30 \div 5 = 7$ c. $24 \div 4 = 6$
   - **(b.)** $32 \div 4 = 8$ d. $77 \div 11 = 7$

2. Fill in the box. $49 \div \boxed{9} = 7$

3. Fill in the box. $30 \div 6 = \boxed{5}$

4. Fill in the box. $\boxed{9} = 72 \div 9$

5. Fill in the box. $42 \div 7 = \boxed{6}$

6. Fill in the box. $\boxed{48} \div 4 = 12$

7. Fill in the box. $55 \div \boxed{5} = 11$

8. Fill in the box. $54 \div 6 = \boxed{8}$

9. Fill in the box. $56 \div 7 = \boxed{9}$

10. Fill in the box. $36 \div \boxed{6} = 6$

11. Fill in the box. $\boxed{81} \div 9 = 9$

12. Fill in the box. $\boxed{48} \div 2 = 24$

13. Fill in the box. $40 \div \boxed{8} = 5$

14. Which answer is NOT correct?
    - a. $24 \div 8 = 3$ **(c.)** $40 \div 5 = 9$
    - b. $28 \div 7 = 4$ d. $36 \div 9 = 4$

15. Fill in the box. $48 \div \boxed{8} = 6$

16. Fill in the box. $\boxed{63} \div 7 = 9$

17. Fill in the box. $64 \div \boxed{8} = 8$

18. Which is NOT correct?
    - **(a.)** $36 \div 3 = 13$ b. $27 \div 3 = 9$

19. Fill in the box. $81 \div \boxed{8} = 9$

20. Which is correct?
    - a. $18 \div 3 = 6$ b. $20 \div 4 = 5$

Fourth Grade Book of Math Tests   Copyright ©2000 by Incentive Publications, Inc., Nashville, TN.

The baseball fans love to buy food and souvenirs to support their team.
Use the price sign to solve problems 21–23.

FOOD & OTHER GOOD STUFF

Hot Dogs	$ 2	Hats	$ 11
Soda Pop	$ 1	Pennants	$ 3
Popcorn	$ 1	Sweatshirts	$ 21
Pizza	$ 4	Pom Poms	$ 5
Tacos	$ 2	T-Shirts	$ 16

24. Compute:
93,048 ÷ 8

Answer: _____

21. Rufus spent **$72** on pizza.
How many slices did he buy?

Answer: _____

22. Georgia's family bought **9** of
something. They spent **$144.**
What item did they buy?

Answer: _____

25. Is this answer correct?
(Circle yes or no.)
927 ÷ 4 = 236
yes   **no**

26. What is the missing number?

1806 ÷ _____ = 7

23. A group of fans bought **2** tacos
and **2** hot dogs each. They spent
$184. How many fans were in
the group?

Answer: _____

27. What is the correct answer?
467 ÷ 8 = _____

A. 59
B. 58 with a remainder of 3
C. 60 with a remainder of 7

Name
_____

Fourth Grade Book of Math Tests

129 baseball players rode to a tournament in six-passenger mini-vans. *(Each van held 6 passengers in addition to the drivers. No players were drivers.)*

28. How many vans did they fill completely? _____

29. How many players were left (the remainder)? _____

30. Compute:

$$28 \overline{)786}$$

31. Circle the problems that have correct answers.

    A. **4200 ÷ 70 = 60**

    B. **560 ÷ 90 = 40**

    C. **24,000 ÷ 300 = 800**

    D. **200 ÷ 50 = 40**

    E. **630 ÷ 70 = 9**

32. Max has kept track of his hits the entire time of his baseball career. He has gotten a base hit **864** times. If he has played **12** seasons, how many hits has he averaged in each season?

Answer: _____

33. Georgio drinks **18** quarts of water each week at games and practices. He is trying to figure out how many weeks it took him to drink **778** quarts. Did he do the problem right? *(Circle yes or no.)*

yes   **no**

Name _____

Fourth Grade Book of Math Tests

34. Compute:

$$511 \overline{)14,308}$$

35. Is this problem solved correctly?
(Circle yes or no.)

yes

no

$$403 \overline{)41,106} \quad 102$$

36. Solve the problem to find **n**.

$$4,000\ n = 80$$

n = _____

37. Solve the problem to find x.

$$738 \div x = 9$$

x = _____

38. The baseball coach has **987** winning games on his record. He has been coaching for **19** seasons. Estimate the number of wins per season.

Your estimate: _____

39. All the players on the team needed new baseball gloves. They spent a total of **$2478** on gloves. Each glove cost **$59**. Estimate the number of players.

Your estimate: _____

40. The members of the baseball team have worn out **900** pairs of shoes. There are **28** players. Estimate the number of pairs worn out by each player.

Your estimate: _____

Name _____

33

ALL OPERATIONS

Name _____   Possible Correct Answers: 30

Date _____   Your Correct Answers: _____

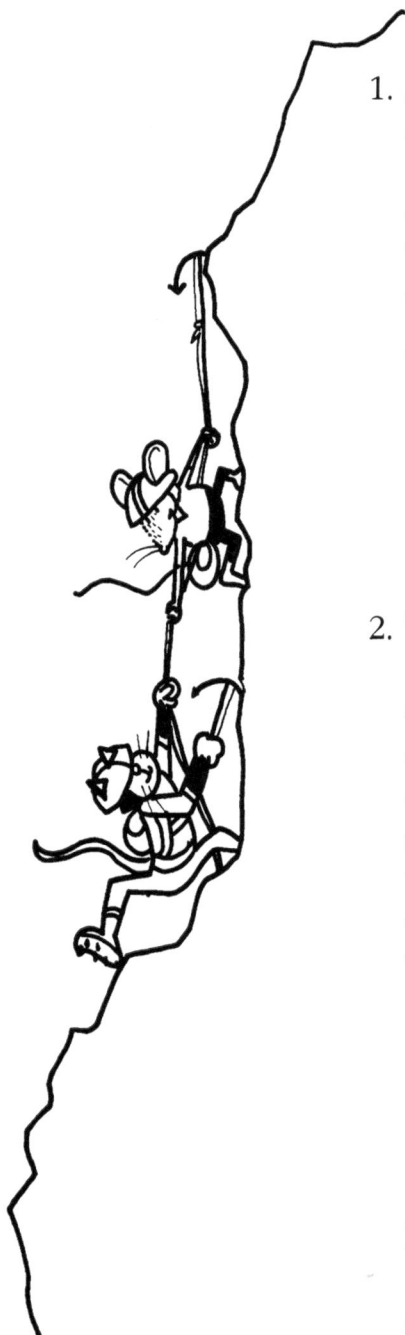

1. A group of mountain climbers carried a total of **294** pounds of gear. Each one carried **42** pounds. To find out how many climbers were in the group, you would:

   A. add
   B. subtract
   C. multiply
   D. divide

2. The climbers climbed **1200** feet the first day. On the second day, they climbed **1800** feet. On day three, they climbed another **700** feet to the top. To find out the total distance they climbed to the top, you would:

   A. add
   B. subtract
   C. multiply
   D. divide

   Find the answer:

   _____

3. They started out carrying **54** pounds of food all together. By the time they were ready to head down from the summit, they had **17** pounds of food left. To find out how much food they used on the upward climb, you would:

   A. add
   B. subtract
   C. multiply
   D. divide

4. Before starting this climb, the friends had done lots of running to get into shape. They each ran about **35** miles a week for **22** weeks. To find out the distance each climber ran before the climb, you would:

   A. add
   B. subtract
   C. multiply
   D. divide

   Find the answer:

   _____

Fourth Grade Book of Math Tests

Fill in each box with **+**, **−**, **x**, or **÷**.

5. $368 \boxed{} 68 = 300$

6. $4,500 \boxed{} 50 = 90$

7. $21,000 \boxed{} 3,000 = 7$

8. $336 \boxed{} 6 = 56$

9. $24,000 \boxed{} 50 = 24,050$

10. $62 \boxed{} 100 = 6,200$

11. $93,529 \boxed{} 92,529 = 1,000$

12. When the hikers began their climb, the mountain had **56** inches of snow. During the next three weeks, it snowed three times: **5** inches, **12** inches, and **10** inches. Then the warm weather melted about **24** inches away. To find the amount of snow left, you would

   A. add, then add again

   B. add, then subtract

   C. add, then multiply

   D. subtract, then add

13. Three groups of hikers each have **9** members. They all gather at the side of a rushing stream. There is only one log crossing the stream, and only one hiker can cross at a time. It takes **54** minutes for all the hikers to get across the stream. To find out how much time it takes for each one to cross, you would

   A. add, then multiply

   B. divide, them multiply

   C. multiply, then divide

   D. multiply, then subtract

Solve these problems:

14. $95 + 13 - 12 = \boxed{}$

15. $5,000 - 3,000 \times 4 = \boxed{}$

16. $320 + 80 - 10 = \boxed{}$

17. $94 + 6 \div 100 = \boxed{}$

Fourth Grade Book of Math Tests

Use the chart at right for problems 18–22.

A group of climbers kept a record of their progress each day for six days. Some of the information is missing. Fill the information in the chart as you find it by solving the problems.

Record of Our Climb

Monday	950 ft
Tuesday	1,000 ft
Wednesday	
Thursday	450 ft
Friday	
Saturday	

18. On Friday, the group climbed 3 times the distance they climbed on Thursday. How far did they climb on Friday?

Answer: _____

19. The distance climbed on Wednesday was twice the distance climbed on Thursday. How far did they climb on Wednesday?

Answer: _____

21. How much further did they climb on Monday and Tuesday than on Wednesday and Thursday?

Answer: _____

20. The climb was 5,300 feet all together. They reached the top on Saturday. How far did they have left to climb on Saturday?

Answer: _____

22. On Friday, the group climbed an average of 225 feet each hour. How many hours did they climb?

Answer: _____

Name _____

Fourth Grade Book of Math Tests

23. If you were asked to solve this problem, what would you do first?

   $$5 \times (36 + 12) - 10 =$$

   A. multiply by the 5
   B. subtract the 10
   C. add the 36 and 12

24. Solve the problem to find **n**.

   $$49{,}918 + n = 50{,}000$$

   n = _____

25. Solve the problem to find **x**.

   $$110 \div x = 55$$

   x = _____

26. Solve the problem to find **y**.

   $$630 \div y = 70$$

   y = _____

27. Solve the problem to find **n**.

   $$n - 53 = 1$$

   n = _____

28. Rufus and Reggie drank **5** quarts of water each day they climbed. Elmo, Gigi, and Georgia each drank **4** quarts. The friends climbed **19** days during the summer. Estimate the number of quarts they drank all together.

   Your estimate: _____

29. **12,784** hikers and climbers have reported seeing an unusual creature such as Bigfoot or the Abominable Snowman while they were hiking in a mountain area. Only **4,022** of the hikers were positive about what they saw. Estimate the number who were not sure.

   Your estimate: _____

30. Each hiker that climbed Mt. Blister this summer came home with an average of **12** blisters. **790** blisters developed on the feet that climbed Mt. Blister during the summer. Estimate the number of climbers.

   Your estimate: _____

Name _____

Fourth Grade Book of Math Tests

FRACTIONS

Name _____

Possible Correct Answers: 50

Date _____

Your Correct Answers: _____

Circle the correct fraction to answer the question about the picture above.

1. What fraction of the players are taller than number 14?

   $\frac{1}{5}$ $\frac{4}{5}$ $\frac{2}{5}$ $\frac{3}{5}$

2. What fraction of the players are wearing sweat bands?

   $\frac{1}{5}$ $\frac{4}{5}$ $\frac{2}{5}$ $\frac{3}{5}$

3. What fraction of the feet have shoes?

   $\frac{1}{2}$ $\frac{2}{10}$ $\frac{4}{10}$ $\frac{3}{5}$ $\frac{9}{10}$

4. What fraction of the hands are holding basketballs?

   $\frac{3}{10}$ $\frac{1}{5}$ $\frac{3}{5}$ $\frac{4}{5}$ $\frac{1}{2}$

5. What fraction of the players are shorter than number 81?

   $\frac{1}{5}$ $\frac{4}{5}$ $\frac{2}{5}$ $\frac{3}{5}$

6. What fraction of the shoes have untied laces?

   $\frac{2}{5}$ $\frac{2}{10}$ $\frac{3}{5}$ $\frac{1}{9}$ $\frac{8}{9}$

7. Write a fractional numeral to match the words.

   five sixths _____

8. Write a fractional numeral to match the words.

   two thirds _____

9. Write a fractional numeral to match the words.

   eight ninths _____

10. Write a fractional numeral to match the words.

    six and two tenths _____

11. Write a fractional numeral to match the words.

    twenty-one and one third

    _____

12. Write the name of the number in words.

    $\frac{3}{4}$ _____

13. Write the name of the number in words.

    $\frac{7}{8}$ _____

14. Write the name of the number in words.

    $\frac{4}{9}$ _____

15. Write the name of the number in words.

    $4\frac{1}{3}$ _____

16. Write the name of the number in words.

    $16\frac{3}{7}$ _____

17. Circle the largest fraction.

18. Draw a box around the smallest fraction.

$\frac{5}{6}$ $\frac{4}{5}$ $\frac{1}{2}$ $\frac{1}{16}$

$\frac{2}{9}$ $\frac{1}{3}$ $\frac{15}{16}$ $\frac{3}{4}$

Name _____

Fourth Grade Book of Math Tests

19. Put these fractions in order from smallest to largest. Write them on the line above.

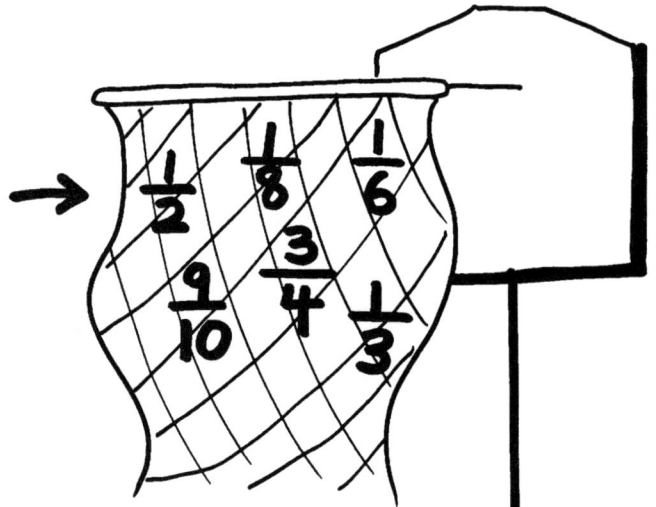

Fractions shown: $\frac{1}{2}$ $\frac{1}{8}$ $\frac{1}{6}$ $\frac{9}{10}$ $\frac{3}{4}$ $\frac{1}{3}$

20. Alvira drank a half gallon of Sweat Quencher drink after the game. Gigi drank $\frac{6}{7}$ of a gallon. Who drank more?

Answer: _____

21. The coach sent Reggie in to play $\frac{1}{16}$ of the game tonight. Elmo played $\frac{1}{5}$ of the game. Who played the least amount of time?

Answer: _____

22. Before the game, The Comets found that $\frac{5}{7}$ of their basketballs were out of air. The Tornadoes found that $\frac{5}{16}$ of their basketballs had no air. Which team had more flat basketballs?

Answer: _____

23. In last week's game, $\frac{2}{3}$ of the starting players were injured. In tonight's game, $\frac{2}{9}$ of the players were injured. For which game were fewer players injured?

Answer: _____

24. Circle the fractions that are in lowest terms.

$\frac{6}{9}$ $\frac{12}{15}$ $\frac{2}{3}$ $\frac{2}{5}$ $\frac{5}{6}$ $\frac{4}{20}$ $\frac{3}{7}$ $\frac{2}{10}$

Name _____

Fourth Grade Book of Math Tests

The basketball team is having a great cheese party after winning the big game. Use the pictures to answer the questions.

25. What fraction of the cheese is left?

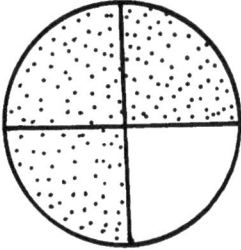

Answer: _____

26. What fraction of the cheese has been eaten?

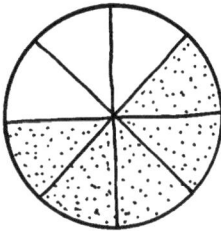

Answer: _____

Cheese Wheel

27. Write a mixed numeral to show how much cheese is left.

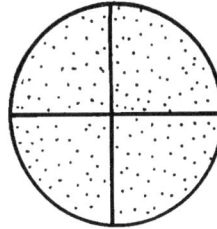

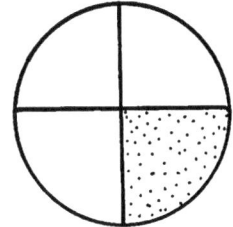

Answer: _____

28. $\frac{2}{3}$ of Elmo's cheese has been eaten. Write two different fractions that stand for the same amount Elmo has eaten (fractions that are equivalent to $\frac{2}{3}$).

_____   _____

29. A basketball player missed $\frac{1}{4}$ of the games with a bad case of rat poisoning. Which fractions are equivalent to this amount? Circle them.

$\frac{5}{20}$ $\frac{3}{12}$ $\frac{1}{2}$ $\frac{6}{10}$ $\frac{2}{8}$ $\frac{2}{10}$ $\frac{4}{16}$

30. Write this fraction in lowest terms: $\frac{12}{16}$ _____

31. Write this fraction in lowest terms: $\frac{2}{24}$ _____

32. Write this fraction in lowest terms: $\frac{6}{9}$ _____

Name _____   41   _____

Fourth Grade Book of Math Tests

34. Write $\frac{19}{6}$ as a mixed numeral.

_____

35. Write $4\frac{1}{2}$ as a fraction.

_____

36. Rufus has been playing basketball for $10\frac{5}{6}$ years. Write this amount of time as an improper fraction.

_____

37. A series of basketball camps has lasted $8\frac{4}{7}$ weeks. Write this as a fraction.

_____

33. Write $\frac{23}{7}$ as a mixed numeral.

_____

Solve these problems.

38. $\frac{4}{9} + \frac{1}{9} - \frac{3}{9} =$ _____

39. $\frac{9}{5} + \frac{3}{5} - \frac{4}{5} =$ _____

40. $\frac{2}{6} + \frac{1}{3} =$ _____

41. $\frac{7}{8} - \frac{3}{5} =$ _____

42. The first game lasted $\frac{2}{3}$ of an hour. The second game lasted $\frac{3}{4}$ of an hour. Francis calculated that the second game was $\frac{1}{3}$ hour longer than the first.

Is she right?_____

43. Write the answer in lowest terms.

$\frac{5}{8} - \frac{3}{6} =$ _____

Name _____

Fourth Grade Book of Math Tests

44. Which answer is correct?

$$\frac{2}{3} \times \frac{1}{2} = \underline{\hspace{1cm}}$$

    A. $\frac{4}{3}$ C. $\frac{3}{4}$

    B. $\frac{2}{6}$ D. none of these

45. Which answer is correct?

$$\frac{6}{7} \times \frac{2}{5} = \underline{\hspace{1cm}}$$

    A. $\frac{35}{14}$

    B. $\frac{35}{12}$

    C. $\frac{12}{35}$

    D. none of these

46. Find the answer.
Write it in lowest terms.

$$\frac{3}{10} \div \frac{5}{2} = \underline{\hspace{1cm}}$$

47. The answer to a problem is $\frac{12}{10}$.
What is the problem?

    A. $\frac{4}{5} \div \frac{3}{2} = \underline{\hspace{1cm}}$

    B. $\frac{4}{5} \div \frac{2}{3} = \underline{\hspace{1cm}}$

    C. $\frac{6}{5} \div \frac{1}{2} = \underline{\hspace{1cm}}$

    D. none of these

48. The age of a basketball player is **15**. Her teammate, Victoria, is $\frac{2}{3}$ of her age. How old is Victoria?

Answer: _____

49. Gigi has $\frac{4}{5}$ of a bag of Yummy Snacks left. She gives $\frac{1}{2}$ of what is left to Victoria. How much of the bag of Yummy Snacks does Victoria get?

Answer: _____

50. Victoria wore out $17\frac{1}{2}$ pairs of socks in the first half of the season. She wore out $5\frac{1}{2}$ pairs in the second half of the season. How many pairs of socks did she wear out in the whole season?

Answer: _____

    Fourth Grade Book of Math Tests

DECIMALS

Name _____   Possible Correct Answers: 40

Date _____   Your Correct Answers: _____

0.55   0.5   5.05   5.005

50.5   5.5   0.05

Choose the decimal numeral (above) that matches the words.

_____   1. five tenths

_____   2. five hundredths

_____   3. five and five tenths

_____   4. five and five thousandths

_____   5. five and five hundredths

Write the decimal numerals.

_____   6. nine thousandths

_____   7. nine and nine tenths

_____   8. ninety-nine and nine tenths

_____   9. nine hundredths

_____   10. nine hundred and nine tenths

11. In the following numeral, what number is in the tenths place?

53.277 _____

12. In the following numeral, what number is in the thousandths place?

6.4905 _____

13. In the following numeral, what number is in the hundredths place?

298.142 _____

14. In the following numeral, what number is in the thousandths place?

82.5091 _____

15. In the following numeral, what number is in the tenths place?

63.76 _____

44

Skaters' Scores

Winnie	5.97
Minnie	5.77
Millie	5.05
Gigi	5.88
Tina	5.96
Lilly	5.19
Ginni	5.79

18. Round Alvira's number to the nearest tenth.

9.073

Answer: _____

16. The scores in the chart above are out of order. Write the names of the skaters in order by their score, from the lowest to the highest score.

A. _____

B. _____

C. _____

D. _____

E. _____

F. _____

G. _____

19. Round this number to the nearest tenth.

5.0792

Answer: _____

20. Round this number to the nearest hundredth.

100.588

Answer: _____

17. Which of the following is in the correct order (from smallest to largest)?

A. 0.05, 7.506, 0.53, 0.34, 7.056

B. 7.506, 0.05, 0.34, 0.53, 7.056

C. 0.05, 7.506, 7.056, 0.53, 0.34,

D. 0.05, 0.34, 0.53, 7.056, 7.506

Name _____

45

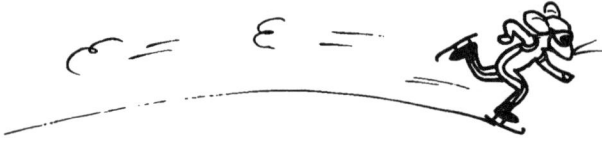

21. Choose the correct answer.

4.33 x 0.1 = _____

    A.   43.3

    B.   433.3

    C.   0.433

    D.   400.33

22. Compute:

$$\begin{array}{r} \$\ 258.57 \\ -\ 52.42 \\ \hline \end{array}$$

23. Compute:

$$\begin{array}{r} \$\ 444.05 \\ +\ 397.85 \\ \hline \end{array}$$

Choose the decimal that matches each fraction. Write the decimal on the line.

_____ 24. $\frac{2}{100}$

_____ 25. $\frac{2}{10}$

_____ 26. $\frac{3}{4}$

_____ 27. $\frac{1}{4}$

_____ 28. $\frac{1}{2}$

_____ 29. $\frac{46}{100}$

_____ 30. $\frac{2}{1000}$

_____ 31. $\frac{34}{100}$

_____ 32. $\frac{7}{10}$

A.   0.75

B.   0.002

C.   0.007

D.   0.2

E.   0.25

F.   0.46

G.   0.5

H.   0.7

I.   0.34

J.   0.02

Name _____

Fourth Grade Book of Math Tests

33. Which percentages are correctly matched with fractions? Circle those that are correct.

A. $\frac{3}{4}$ 75%

B. 5/100   50%

C. 6/10   6%

D. $\frac{1}{4}$ 25%

34. Which percentages are correctly matched with decimals? Circle those that are correct.

A. 0.5   5%

B. 0.85   85%

C. 0.12   12%

D. 0.33   3.3%

35. What number is **three tenths** less than **49.6**?

Answer: _____

36. What number is **five hundredths** more than **81.23**?

Answer: _____

37. Write **0.55** as a percent. _____

38. Gigi's coach used a stopwatch to time her spins. One spin lasted **36.245** seconds. The next spin lasted **5 hundredths** of a second longer. How long was the second spin?

Answer: _____

39. The temperature at an outdoor skating competition was very chilly. At 8 a.m. it was **18.5 degrees** Fahrenheit. By 10 A.M., the temperature had dropped **1.25 degrees**. How cold was it at 10:00?

Answer: _____

40. By six o'clock in the evening, the temperature had fallen to **12.75 degrees** from **12.97 degrees**. Which is the best estimate of the drop in temperature?

A. 2 degrees

B. 0.9 degree

C. 0.02 degree

D. 0.2 degree

Name _____

47

ALGEBRA CONCEPTS

Name _____ Possible Correct Answers: 30

Date _____ Your Correct Answers: _____

1. Write the temperatures in order from coldest to warmest.

_____ °

_____ °

_____ °

_____ °

_____ °

_____ °

_____ °

_____ °

Temperatures at Mt. Awesome

12-1 . . . 16°
12-4 . . . -30°
12-30 . . . 4°
1-1 . . . -28°
1-17 . . . -3°
1-30 . . . 40°
2-5 . . . -16°
2-24 . . . -21°

Compare the amounts on both sides of the box. Write the words *less than*, *greater than*, or *equal to* for each example.

2. **90 x 1** [ ] **90 ÷ 1**

3. **4 x 10** [ ] **6 x 9**

Compare the amounts on both sides of the box. Write **<** *(for less than)*, **>** *(for greater than)*, or **=** *(for equal to)* in each box.

4. **400 + 150** [ ] **1000 – 500**

5. **– 30** [ ] **20**

6. **2 x 14** [ ] **7 x 4**

7. **– 16** [ ] **– 14**

8. **84 ÷ 6** [ ] **110 ÷ 11**

9. **– 30** [ ] **0**

10. **4 x 12** [ ] **220 – 200**

Fourth Grade Book of Math Tests   Copyright ©2000 by Incentive Publications, Inc., Nashville, TN.

Circle one answer for each problem.

---

11. Abby skied **110** meters. Gigi skied twice as far as Abby. Which math expression represents Gigi's distance?

   A. 110 – 110

   B. 110 x 2

   C. 110 + 2

14. Elmo's sled traveled 950 feet across a field. Mario's sled went 500 feet farther. Which math expression shows the distance for Mario's sled?

   A. 950 + 500

   B. 950 – 500

   C. 950 x 500

---

12. What does this math expression mean?

$$15 + n$$

   A the product of a 15 and a number

   B. the sum of 15 and a number

   C. the difference between 15 and number

15. Which math expression matches this?

three times the difference between a number and 100

   A. 3 x n + 100

   B. 3 – n x 100

   C. 3 (n – 100)

---

13. What does this math expression mean?

$$2 (n + 6)$$

   A. the sum of 2, 6, and another number

   B. 2 times the sum of a number and 6

   C. the product of 2 and a number

16. Which math expression (below) means the same as this one?

$$n + 13 – 4 = 19$$

   A. n + 17 = 19

   B. n + 9 = 19

   C. 13 – n + 4 = 19

Name

Fourth Grade Book of Math Tests

17. A snowboarder took 28 hard falls during her practice on Monday. The total number of her falls for Monday and Tuesday was 58. What math equation represents the number that is the total of her falls?

    A. $58 - 28 = n$

    B. $n - 28 = 58$

    C. $58 \div n = 28$

    D. $28 + n = 58$

18. Rufus won 4 medals in the competition. Reggie won 3 medals. Their friend Alfredo also won some medals. The total of all the medals was 15.

    Write an equation (math sentence) to represent the total of their medals. *(You do not have to solve the problem.)*

    _____

19. Two members of the Snow Kings Team, Flo and Moe, spent several hours making snowballs for the big snowball-throwing contest. Ned and Fred spent 4 hours making snowballs for another team. Their time was $\frac{1}{2}$ the amount of time that Flo and Moe worked.

    Which equation should you use to find out how much time Flo and Moe spent making snowballs?

    A. $2 \times n = 4$ B. $2 \times 4 = n$ C. $n + 2 = 4$

20. How long did Flo and Moe work? _____

21. Solve the equation for **n**.

    $$7 \times n = 0$$

    $$n = \underline{\hspace{2cm}}$$

22. Solve the equation for **b**.

    $$b + 12 = 21$$

    $$b = \underline{\hspace{2cm}}$$

23. Solve the equation for **y**.

    $$36 \div y = 4$$

    $$y = \underline{\hspace{2cm}}$$

24. Solve the equation for **d**.

    $$145 - d = 100$$

    $$d = \underline{\hspace{2cm}}$$

Name _____

Fourth Grade Book of Math Tests

In a snowboard competition, the first snowboarder fell 3 times. The second boarder fell 2 times. The third boarder fell as many times as the first two together. What was the total of all the falls?

25. What operation should be used to solve the problem? (Circle one.)
    A. addition
    B. subtraction
    C. multiplication
    D. division

26. Which math equation should be used to find the answer to the question? (Circle one.)
    A. $3 + 2 + 2 = n$
    B. $2(3 + 2) = n$
    C. $2 + 3 + (3 + 2) = n$

27. Solve the equation to find the answer: _____

At the end of a close ski race, the winner of the race divided the prize money equally between herself and each of the other skiers. There were 7 skiers, including the winner. Each skier got $50. How much was the total prize?

28. What operation should be used to solve the problem? (Circle one.)
    A. addition
    B. subtraction
    C. multiplication
    D. division

29. Which math equation should be used to find the answer to the question? (Circle one.)
    A. $7 \times 50 = n$
    B. $50 \div 7 = n$
    C. $7 + 50 = n$

30. Solve the equation to find the answer: _____

Name _____

51

Fourth Grade Book of Math Tests

Problem Solving Skills Checklists

Problem-Solving Test # 1:

APPROACHES TO PROBLEMS

Test Location: pages 54–57

Skill	*Test Items*
Identify or define a problem	1–3
Identify information unnecessary for problem solution	4–5
Identify information needed for problem solution	6–10
Describe information that is missing from a problem	11–14
Identify operations needed for problem solution	15–18
Identify order of operations needed for problem solution	19–20

Problem-Solving Test # 2:

PROBLEM-SOLVING STRATEGIES

Test Location: pages 58–61

Skill	*Test Items*
Translate a problem into an equation	1–3
Choose the correct formula to solve a problem	4–8
Extend a pattern to solve a problem	9–10
Estimate problem solutions	11–12
Make a diagram or chart to solve a problem	13–14
Use mental math to solve a problem	15–16
Use logic to solve a problem	15–16
Solve a problem with trial and error	17–18
Select an appropriate strategy for solving a given problem	19–20

Problem-Solving Test # 3 and Test # 4:

PROBLEMS TO SOLVE

Test Location: pages 62–67 and pages 68–73

Skill	Test	Test Items
Solve a variety of word problems	# 3	1–5
Solve problems with whole numbers	# 3	1–4, 12–22, 29–30
Solve problems using information from charts and tables	# 3	6–11, 12–16
Solve problems with fractions	# 3	5, 21, 29, 30
Find solutions to equations	# 3	17–22
Solve problems involving money	# 3	6–11, 33–40
Solve problems using decimals	# 3	23–25
Solve problems involving time	# 3	26–28
Solve problems with rate	# 3	31, 32
Use a diagram or illustration to assist with problem solution	# 3	34–40
Use formulas to find perimeter of plane figures	# 4	1–3
Use formulas to find area of plane figures	# 4	4–5
Use formulas to find volume or capacity of space figures	# 4	6–7
Solve consumer problems involving discounts	# 4	8–10
Solve problems with percent	# 4	8–10
Solve problems using information from a graph	# 4	11–16
Choose appropriate approach to problems	# 4	17–20
Use logic to solve a problem	# 4	17–21
Solve probability problems	# 4	22–25
Find combinations or permutations to solve problems	# 4	26–27
Determine the accuracy of problem solutions	# 4	28–30

Problem-Solving Test # 5:

PROBLEM SOLVING PROCESS

Test Location: pages 74–77

Skill

The problem solving process test is a test of problem solving performance. A scoring guide (page 137) is used to enable the adult to give students a score of 1–5 in the areas of Conceptual Understanding, Strategies & Processes, Communication, Correctness (Accuracy, and Verification of the answer.

Fourth Grade Book of Math Tests

APPROACHES TO PROBLEMS

Name _____   Possible Correct Answers: 20

Date _____   Your Correct Answers: _____

Read the numbered paragraphs below (1–3). Decide if each paragraph has everything it needs to be a problem. If the paragraph is a problem that can be solved, mark an X in front of it. (*Do not solve the problems.*)

_____ 1. Our football team, the Chargers, moved the ball forward 47 yards on the first play. On the second play, the ball moved forward 23 yards. On the third play, there was a loss of 17 yards.

_____ 2. Rufus and Elmo slept on the long bus ride home from the game. Between the two players, they slept $12\frac{1}{2}$ hours. Rufus slept 7 hours. How long did Elmo sleep?

_____ 3. Felix's sports bag weighed 16 pounds. Elmo's bag weighed 4 pounds more. Alfred's bag weighed 7 pounds less than Elmo's. How much did Alfred's bag weigh?

4. Underline any information in the problem below that is NOT needed in order to find the answer. (*Do not solve the problem.*)

During the football season, 20 football players were injured during a game. 15 more of the players were injured during practice. There were 40 players on the team. What fraction of the team members were injured during games?

5. Circle the letter of any line below which contains information that is NOT needed to answer this question:
How many touchdown attempts by the Chargers were the Warriors able to stop?

   A. The Chargers attempted 9 touchdowns.

   B. The Warriors attempted 6 touchdowns.

   C. The Chargers scored 7 touchdowns.

   D. The Warriors scored 3 touchdowns.

Fourth Grade Book of Math Tests

What information is needed to answer each question below? *(Circle the correct letters.)*

6. How many fans were still at the game when the second half began?

Rah - rah - rah

A. 3,940 fans arrived at the beginning.

B. 759 more came during the first half.

C. 290 left before halftime.

D. 1,570 fans ate hot dogs at the game.

E. 301 fans left in the last quarter.

7. What fraction of the players had the flu this week?

A. $\frac{1}{4}$ of the players were injured.

B. 28 players played during the game.

C. The team has 40 players.

D. 8 players had the flu this week.

E. 11 players had the flu last week.

8. How much spaghetti did each player eat?

A. The team ate 36 pounds of spaghetti.

B. Each player ate the same amount.

C. 17 players ate salad with their meals.

D. 12 loaves of bread were eaten.

E. There were 40 players eating spaghetti.

9. What was the final score for the Chargers?

A. Chargers scored 7 points in the 1st half.

B. Warriors scored 10 points in the 1st half.

C. Chargers scored twice as much in the 2nd half as they did in the 1st half.

D. Warriors scored 9 points in the 2nd half.

10. Who won the football game?

A. Chargers scored 7 points in the 1st half.

B. Warriors scored 10 points in the 1st half.

C. Chargers scored twice as much in the 2nd half as they did in the 1st half.

D. Warriors scored 9 points in the 2nd half.

Name _____

55

11. Some information is missing from this problem. Describe the information needed in order to find a solution.

> Fans at the football game drank 485 gallons of hot chocolate. How much more coffee than hot chocolate did the fans drink?

Missing: _____

_____

_____

_____

12. Some information is missing from this problem. Describe the information needed in order to find a solution.

> The number of coaches who worked with the Chargers last year was $\frac{3}{4}$ of the number working with the team this year. How many coaches worked with the Chargers last year?

Missing: _____

_____

_____

_____

13. Some information is missing from this problem. Describe the information needed in order to find a solution.

> The cheerleaders have 16 old cheers that they must learn. How many cheers must a new cheerleader learn to know all the old ones and the new ones?

Missing: _____

_____

_____

_____

14. Some information is missing from this problem. Describe the information needed in order to find a solution.

> During the football season, the coaches have a meeting twice a week. The football season lasts several weeks. How many meetings in all are held during the season?

Missing: _____

_____

_____

_____

15. What operation would be used to solve this problem?
The Chargers' quarterback was knocked down 22 times during the season. This was 10 times fewer than last season. How many times was he knocked down last season?
   A. addition   C. multiplication
   B. subtraction   D. division

Name _____

16. What operation is needed to solve this problem?

> Chargers team members spent $1,450 on doctor and hospital visits this season. There are 40 team members. What was the average cost of hospital and doctor services for each team member?

  A. addition   C. multiplication
  B. subtraction   D. division

17. What operation is needed to solve this problem?

> The equipment for each football player costs $165. There are 40 players on the team. How much is the cost of all the equipment?

  A. addition   C. multiplication
  B. subtraction   D. division

18. What operations are needed to solve this problem?

> The football team has practiced 3 hours on Mondays through Thursdays, and 5 hours on Friday for 16 weeks. What is the total number of hours they have practiced?

  A. addition   C. multiplication
  B. subtraction   D. division

19. What is the correct order for performing operations to solve this problem?

> At the championship game, the fans ate 860 slices of pizza and 1,240 hot dogs. The pizza and hot dogs each cost $3.00. How much did the fans spend on pizza and hot dogs together?

  A. divide, then add
  B. add, then divide
  C. add, then multiply
  D. subtract, then multiply

20. What operation should be performed first in order to solve this problem?

> After the game, the coaches cooked pizzas for the 40 players on the team. They baked 36 pizzas. 9 of the pizzas were burned. The team members shared the rest of the pizzas. How much pizza did each player get?

  A. addition   C. multiplication
  B. subtraction   D. division

Name

57

PROBLEM-SOLVING STRATEGIES

Name _____   Possible Correct Answers: 20

Date _____   Your Correct Answers: _____

1. To solve a problem, it is often helpful to write an equation so you can see what needs to be done. Choose the right equation for finding the answer to this problem.

   A team of bikers spent $9000 on new bikes. They each spent $450.

   How many bikers were on the team?

   A. $9000 − n = $450

   B. $450 x $9000 = n

   C. $450 + n = $9000

   D. $9000 ÷ $450 = n

2. Choose the best equation for solving this problem.

   20 mountain bikers started riding to the top of the mountain. 6 stopped from injuries. 3 more stopped because of bike problems. 2 of the bikers fixed their bikes and continued.

   How many bikers got to the top?

   A. 20 + 6 + 3 + 2 = n

   B. 20 − 6 − 3 + 2 = n

   C. 20 + 3 x 2 + 6 = n

   D. 2 x 6 + 2 x 20 = n

3. Write an equation that will help you find the answer to this problem. Then solve the equation.

   The bikers drank 1,869 quarts of water on a hot day of the bike race. Each biker drank 3 quarts.

   How many bikers were in the race?

   Your equation:

   _____

   Your answer:

   _____

58

The bikers practice on courses of all shapes. Use a formula to find the distance around the outside (perimeter) of this figure.

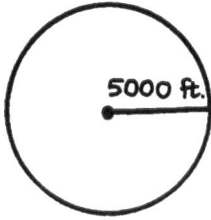
5000 ft.

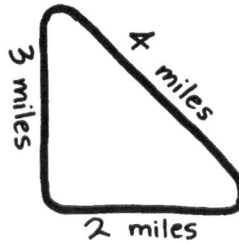
3 miles
4 miles
2 miles

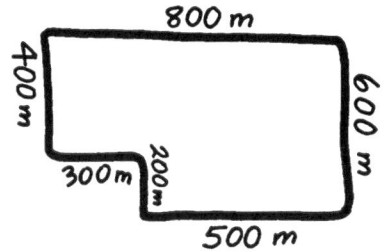
800 m
400 m
300 m
200 m
600 m
500 m

4. P = _____

5. P = _____

6. P = _____

7. A rectangular bike track is 50 feet long and 40 feet wide. What is the area of the space inside the track? Use a formula to find the area.

A = _____

8. Each biker drinks a huge container of sports drink after the race. How much space is inside this container? Use a formula to find the volume in cubic inches.

POWER DRINK
6 in.
4 in.
4 in.

V = _____

9. Find the pattern to solve the problem:

The first week of training, a biker rode $1\frac{1}{2}$ hours. The next week, he rode 2 hours. In Week # 3, he rode $2\frac{1}{2}$ hours. During week # 4, he rode 3 hours. If he follows the same pattern, how much time will he spend riding in Week # 5?

Answer: _____

10. Find the pattern on the signs. Fill in the last sign to keep the pattern going.

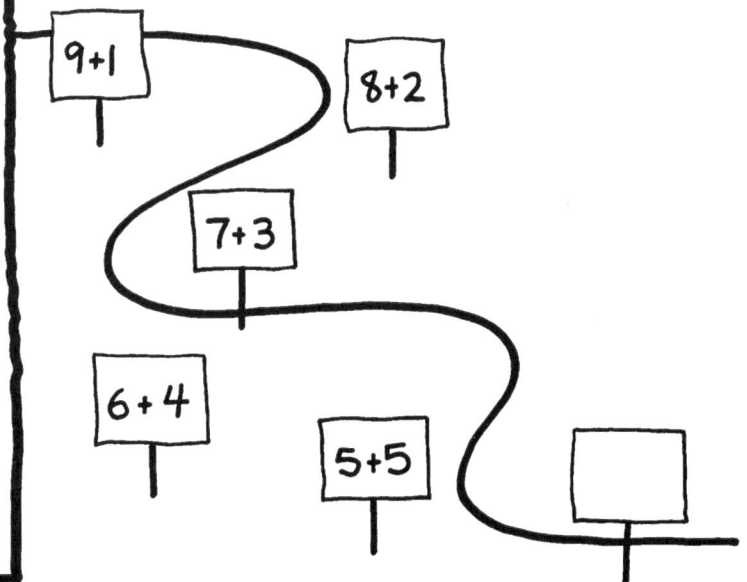
9+1
8+2
7+3
6+4
5+5

11. Estimate the answer:

A mountain biker rides about 290 miles a week. Over a season of 12 weeks, about how far will she ride?

Your estimate: _____

12. Estimate the answer:

Gigi's boxing shoes cost $88. Her jacket cost $49, and her helmet cost $98. About how much is the total cost?

Your estimate: _____

13. Label the diagram to help you find the answer.

The four bikers are Minnie, Winnie, Gigi, and Lilly.

Gigi is on the right end (as you look at the picture).

Lilly is between Minnie and Winnie.

Gigi is not next to Minnie.

Which biker is Minnie?

Minnie is Biker # _____

14. Use mental math to solve this problem:

The bike race began at 8:15 A.M. The last biker finished the race 6 hours and 30 minutes later. What time was it when she finished?

Answer: _____

15. Use mental math to solve this problem:

There were 200 spectators at the race yesterday. Today there were 50 less than twice as many as yesterday. How many spectators watched the race today?

Answer: _____

Name _____

60

16. Use trial and error to solve this problem. (Keep trying different answers to the problem until you find the right one.)

    An even number has two digits. The sum of the digits is 7. The product of the digits is 12.

    What is the number? _____

17. Use trial and error to solve this problem.

    Georgia is 6 years younger than her friend. In 6 years, her friend will be twice the age that Georgia is now. Georgia is less than 20 years old now.

    What is Georgia's age now? _____

18. Use trial and error to solve this problem.

    > Georgia's place in the big race is a 3–digit odd number. None of the digits is the same number. The smallest digit is in the middle. The third digit is the largest. The sum of the digits is 9. One digit is zero. There are no 5s in the number.

    What is the number? _____

19. Choose the best strategy for solving this problem.

    > The bikers race on a round track. The diameter of the circle is 850 feet. How far do the bikers ride when they go around the track one time?

    a) Make a graph.
    b) Use trial and error.
    c) Write a ratio.
    d) Estimate the answer.
    e) Draw a diagram.
    f) Use a formula.

20. Choose the best strategy for solving this problem.

    > After Rufus broke his leg, he missed $\frac{1}{2}$ of the races on a race tour. He missed 16 races all together.

    How many races were on the tour?

    a) Change the problem into an equation.
    b) Make a number line.
    c) Estimate the answer.
    d) Make a graph.
    e) Use logic.
    f) Draw a diagram.

Name _____

61

Fourth Grade Book of Math Tests

PROBLEMS TO SOLVE, PART I

Name _____   Possible Correct Answers: 40

Date _____   Your Correct Answers: _____

1. A hockey player has been in the penalty box 39 times so far this season. On the average, he has been in the box 3 times per game. How many games has he played this year?

Answer: _____

2. The Ice Kings play their home games at the Frozen Corners Arena. The arena has 4,500 seats. The seats are divided into 50 sections. How many seats are in each section?

Answer: _____

4. The number of games that Coach Caspian has coached in his 3–year career is an odd number. The number has three digits. All of them are different, and all are odd numbers. The sum of the digits is 13. The largest digit is in the one's place. The smallest digit is in the hundred's place. There are no 5s in the number. What is the number of games he has coached?

Answer: _____

5. The hockey team was served 21 pizzas after the game. They ate $\frac{2}{3}$ of the amount they were served. How much pizza did they leave uneaten?

Answer: _____

3. These are the numbers of goals the team scored in seven games: 4, 3, 6, 3, 3, 4, and 5. What is the average number of goals scored per game?

Answer: _____

SNOW KINGS TEAM MEMORABILIA

Hats	$9.00	Mugs	$6.50
Sweatshirts	$22.00	Key Chains	$2.50
T-Shirts	$16.50	Bumper Stickers	$3.00
Jackets	$49.90	Pins	$3.00
Blankets	$25.00	Mittens	$7.50

Use the chart to answer questions 6–11.

6. Which 2 items together would cost $47.00? _____

7. Could a fan buy 5 key chains for $10.00? _____

8. How much would it cost to buy a T-shirt and 2 pins? _____

9. What is the difference in price between a jacket and a hat? _____

10. Gigi buys mittens with a $20 bill. How much change will she get? _____

11. What will Mimi pay for 2 mugs and 3 bumper stickers? _____

Use the table to answer questions 12–16.

12. How many games were played each year? _____

13. What was the total number of ties? _____

14. How many games were won from Year # 1 through Year # 4? _____

15. What was the difference between the most wins and the most losses? _____

16. How many losses were there in Year # 8? _____

TEAM RECORD for 8 YEARS

Year	Wins	Losses	Ties
Year # 1	18	10	2
Year # 2	11	16	3
Year # 3	16	13	1
Year # 4	21	5	4
Year # 5	23	5	2
Year # 6	18	8	4
Year # 7	12	18	0
Year # 8	10		3

Name _____

Fourth Grade Book of Math Tests

17. A player spent $450 on tennis lessons. She took 30 lessons. How much did each lesson cost?

Solve the equation for the cost (c).

$$c = \$450 \div 30$$

$$c = \underline{\hspace{2cm}}$$

18. Georgio is 12. His tennis coach is four years older than twice his age. How old is the coach?

Solve the equation for the age (a).

$$a = (2 \times 12) + 4$$

$$a = \underline{\hspace{2cm}}$$

19. Solve the equation for d.

$$25\, d = 450$$

$$d = \underline{\hspace{2cm}}$$

20. Winnie lost 270 tennis balls last month. The balls are sold in cans of 3. How many cans of tennis balls did Winnie lose? Solve the equation for the number of cans (n).

$$270 \div 3 = n$$

$$\underline{\hspace{2cm}} = n$$

21. Solve the equation for x.

$$\frac{1}{2} + \frac{1}{4} = x$$

$$\underline{\hspace{2cm}} = x$$

22. Elmo practiced 74 hours this week. Last week he practiced 16 hours less. How many hours did he practice last week? Solve the equation for the number of hours (h).

$$74 - 16 = h$$

$$\underline{\hspace{2cm}} = h$$

Name _____

Fourth Grade Book of Math Tests

23. After school each day, Georgia travels to the tennis courts for practice. The distance from her school to the tennis courts and back to her home is 2.5 miles. She does this five days a week. What is the distance she travels in a week?

Answer: _____

24. Sometimes Lilly jogs one mile to the tennis court for exercise. Today, she jogged the distance in 10.3 minutes. Millie jogged the same distance in a time that was 2.2 minutes faster. How much time did it take Millie?

Answer: _____

25. Thirty-five players from Georgia's team took part in the tennis match today. 0.8 of the players were winners. How many players won their matches?

Answer: _____

26. The tennis team traveled for 6 hours and 20 minutes to get to a tournament. They left home at 3:10 p.m. What time did they arrive at the tournament location?

Answer: _____

27. The tennis tournament began at 9:30 a.m. The last match finished 4 hours and 35 minutes later. What time did the tournament end?

Answer: _____

28. The trip home began at 11:35 a.m. The team arrived at home at 6:10 p.m. How long did the trip take?

Answer: _____

Fourth Grade Book of Math Tests

29. The soccer bag with all Elmo's clothes and junk weighed $10\frac{1}{2}$ pounds. He let his friend Rufus put some stuff in the bag. This added $4\frac{1}{3}$ pounds to the bag. How much did the bag weigh after Rufus put his stuff in it?

Answer: _____

30. After practice, Reggie gave $\frac{3}{4}$ of his pizza to his two friends. Each of them ate half of what Reggie had given away. How much pizza did each friend eat?

Answer: _____

31. Oscar scored 3 goals in the first 4 games of the season. At this rate, how many goals would Oscar score in 12 games?

Answer: _____

32. The Comet's goalie stopped 9 shots on goal in the first 10 minutes of the game. At this rate, how many goals would she stop in the 40–minute game?

Answer: _____

33. New shoes for the whole soccer team cost $792.00. The team has 16 members. How much did each pair of shoes cost?

Answer: _____

34. $425.50 worth of tickets to the soccer game were sold ahead of time. Tickets sold at the game brought in $879.75. How much money was earned from ticket sales all together?

Answer: _____

Name _____

Fourth Grade Book of Math Tests

35. What was the total cost of the shoes and socks?

_____

36. How many sweatbands could Caspian buy for $15.00?

_____

37. How much more was spent for the shoes than for the ball?

_____

38. How much did Caspian pay for his shirt, shorts, and shoes?

_____

39. What would it cost for the whole team of 19 members to buy socks?

_____

40. Caspian bought two shirts. How much change did he get from three $20 bills?

_____

Sweat-band $2.50

Shirt $23.50

Shorts $26.00

Socks $7.95

Shoes $79.50

Soccer ball $19.25

Fourth Grade Book of Math Tests

PROBLEMS TO SOLVE, PART II

Name _____   Possible Correct Answers: 30

Date _____   Your Correct Answers: _____

1. An inner tube has a diameter of 40 inches. What is its circumference?

   Circumference = _____

2. A triangular float has sides of these lengths: 4 feet, 3 feet and 5 feet. What is the perimeter?

   Perimeter = _____

3. A swimmer walks around the outer edge of this pond. How far does she walk?

   Perimeter = _____

4. What area does the pond cover? (See the diagram.)

   Area = _____

950 yd.

510 yd.

5. A rectangular raft measures 6 feet by 8 feet. What area does it cover?

   Area = _____

Fourth Grade Book of Math Tests

6. Three friends inflated the float shown below. How much air did the full float contain? *(Give the volume of the float.)*

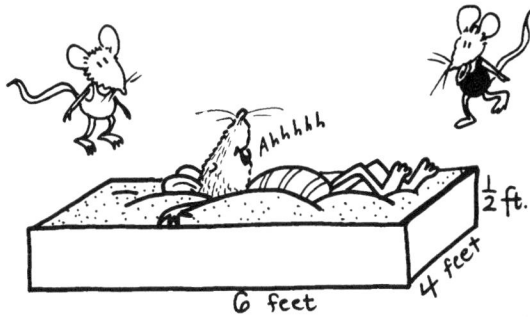

Volume = _____

7. What is the volume of this box of snacks that friends share on the beach?

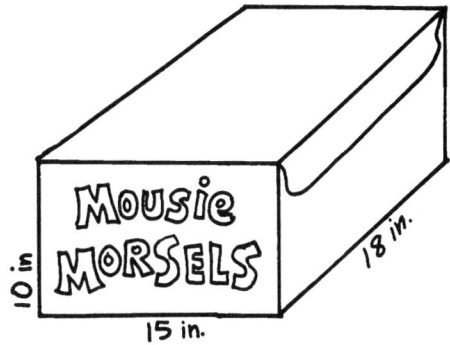

Volume = _____

Caspian got some great discounts on water-skiing equipment. Use the price tags shown to help you solve the problems.

8. He got a 50% discount on the cost of the water-skis.

How much did he pay? _____

9. Caspian saved 20% on the price of a life jacket.

How much did he save? _____

10. Caspian bought a new wakeboard, a new tow rope, and a life jacket. He got a 10% discount on the whole sale.

How much did he pay in all? _____

Water Skis
$130.00

Life Jacket
$80.00

Wake Board
$190.00

TOW ROPE
$16.00

Wet suit
$89.00

Name _____

69

Use the graph to solve problems 11–16.

Successful Water-Ski Jumps
in 6-Competition Series

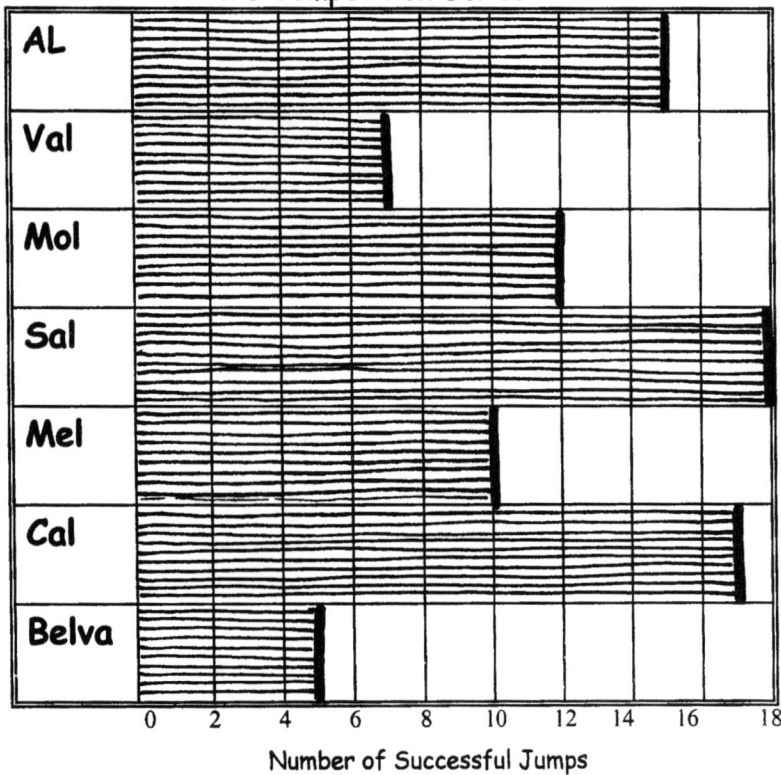

AL	
Val	
Mol	
Sal	
Mel	
Cal	
Belva	

0   2   4   6   8   10   12   14   16   18

Number of Successful Jumps

11. What is the difference between
    the number of most and least successful jumps? _____

12. What is the total number of successful jumps of Cal, Mol, and Mel? _____

13. Who had 6 fewer jumps than Sal? _____

14. Who had less than half as many jumps as Mol? _____

15. How many skiers had more than twice as many successful jumps as Val? _____

16. Who had $\frac{2}{3}$ the number of Al's successful jumps? _____

Name _____

70

Use the illustration and the information to help you solve the logic problem.

Read the information about the skiers and label each skier in the picture with her name.

* Four friends are competing in a water-ski jumping contest.
* Their names are Gigi, Winnie, Minnie, and Ellie.
* Gigi is not next to Winnie.
* Ellie is not wearing a helmet.
* Minnie and Winnie are on 2 skis.
* Gigi is wearing goggles.

Given the information above, which of these statements could be true?

Circle the number of a statement if it could be true.

17. Gigi is skiing on two skis.

18. Winnie is wearing a helmet.

19. Ellie is next to Winnie.

20. Minnie is on two skis.

21. Ellie is next to Gigi.

Fourth Grade Book of Math Tests

22. Every time the rat twins have to row the boat across the lake, they flip a coin to see who has to row. If they flip a penny 10 times, about how many times will it come up "tails"?

    A. 10   B. 20   C. 5   D. none

23. Caspian's closet has 15 fishing poles. 12 of them are red. The rest are white. If Caspian grabs one pole without looking, what is the chance that it will be white?

    A. 12/15   C. 3/15
    B. 12/15   D. 3/12

24. A hungry boater reaches into his picnic basket for a sandwich. The basket holds 6 ham sandwiches and 5 Swiss cheese sandwiches. What are the chances that the sandwich he grabs will be ham?

    A. 6/5   C. 1/6
    B. 6/11   D. 5/11

25. Mario has four sun umbrellas in the boat. They are all white on the outside. On the inside, one is green, one is red, and two are yellow. He grabs an umbrella and opens it. What are the chances that his umbrella is yellow inside?

    A. 2/2   B. 2/1   C. 2/4   D. 3/4

26. Caspian has two kinds of bait: worms and minnows. He puts bait on three lines. How many different combinations of bait can he put on the three lines? Write the combinations on the lines below:

    _____

    _____

    _____

    _____

27. Four friends decide to fish in pairs. The friends are Alfredo, Elmo, Reggie, and Georgio. Name all the possible pairs they could form:

    _____

    _____

    _____

    _____

    _____

Name _____

72

Check the accuracy of the solutions to the problems below. Show the work that you do to find out if an answer is correct. Circle **yes** or **no** to show whether the original answer was correct or not.

28. Mario caught 260 fish last year. He threw $\frac{1}{10}$ of the fish back. Of the ones he kept, he gave 168 away to friends to eat. He put the rest in his freezer. Of these, he has eaten 23. How many fish are left in his freezer?

    The answer is 43 fish.

    Is this correct?   yes   no

29. There are 145 boats on the lake today. Forty percent of them are in shady spots.
    How many boats are in the sun?
    The answer is 58 boats in the sun.

    Is this correct?   yes   no

30. Fishermen tell great stories about the fish they've caught. Mario is a great story teller. Today, he insists he caught a fish that was 239 inches long.
    How long would Mario's fish be, if the measurement were given in feet and inches?
    The answer is 20 feet, 9 inches.

    Is this correct?   yes   no

Name _____

Fourth Grade Book of Math Tests

PROBLEM-SOLVING PROCESS

Name _____　Possible Correct Answers: 25

Date _____　Your Correct Answers: _____

DIRECTIONS:

1) Choose ONE of the problems on page two of this test.

  2) Use the space on pages 3 and 4 to solve the problem.

    3) Show your answer and ALL your work clearly.

      4) Make sure that a reader can tell how you solved the problem. Use diagrams, pictures, symbols, or words to show the steps you went through to solve the problem.

  5) When you finish, review your work and find a way to show that your answer is correct. You might work the problem a second way to show this.

      • Your problem solving will be scored on these five areas.

    • You can receive 1 to 5 points on each trait.

  • A good example of problem solving scores at least 3 points in each area.

UNDERSTANDING of the CONCEPT:
Show that you understand what the problem is, and that you can change the problem into mathematical symbols, numbers, or ideas. Use the important information from the problem that is needed to solve it.

CORRECTNESS:
Give a final answer that is a clear answer to the question asked in the problem. Your final answer needs to be correct.

COMMUNICATION:
Clearly show the process and strategies you used with pictures, symbols, diagrams, and/or words.

STRATEGIES & PROCESSES:
Show all the numbers, diagrams, symbols, equations, or pictures that you used to solve the problem. Show them in the order they were used. The strategies you choose need to be good ones to fit that problem.

VERIFICATION:
After the problem is solved, find another way to solve the problem or to defend your answer.

Problems to Solve (Choose One)

PROBLEM # 1

Ellie took out all of her savings ($180) to shop for softball equipment. She bought a glove for $79, a new bat for $33, gloves for $7.95, and shoes for $58. Then she got $25 for her birthday. She put all the money that she didn't spend back into her savings account. How much did she put back?

PROBLEM # 2

Seven friends went fishing and caught some good-sized fish. The seven fish had an average length of 22 inches. Six of the seven fish lengths were: 18, 20, 22, 19, 26, and 17. What was the length of the seventh fish?

PROBLEM # 3

The track team is taking a supply of energy bars along to the big track meet. Each energy bar measures 4 x 3 x 2 inches. How many bars can they pack into a container that is 12 inches square?

PROBLEM # 4

Some basketball fans are sewing a banner for their school gym. The pattern for the banner is shown below. They are using the school colors of red, blue, and white. Each piece of fabric they have covers 9 square feet. How many pieces of red fabric will they need?

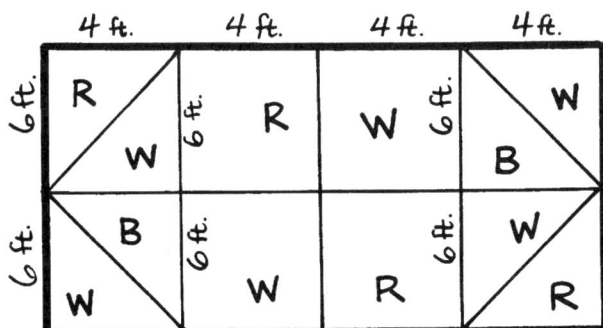

PROBLEM # 5

For exercise, the members of the Net Warriors Volleyball Team, took turns on a stair stepping machine. Winnie used the stepper for 18 minutes, 30 seconds. Gigi took a turn that was $\frac{1}{2}$ hour long. Lilly used the stepper for 1 hour and 15 seconds. Georgia used the machine for twice the length of time as Gigi. How long was the stair stepper used by team members?

PROBLEM # 6

In the snowboard race, there were 4 boarders: Elmo, Rufus, Arlo, and Lou. Elmo finished later than Lou. Rufus finished two boarders behind Elmo. Arlo finished ahead of Rufus. In what order did the runners finish? (Tell who was 1st, 2nd, 3rd, and 4th.)

PROBLEM # 7

Monday's baseball practice was twice as long as Tuesday's. Wednesday's practice was 1 hour longer than Tuesday's. The team practiced a total of 7 hours. How long was Tuesday's practice?

PROBLEM # 8

The gymnastics team left home for a long bus trip to the state meet. They traveled for 10 hours and 20 minutes, arriving at noon on Friday. What time and day did they leave home? (The state meet was in the same time zone as their home.)

Name _____

Name_____

Problem # _____

Use the space on pages 3 and 4 to solve the problem. Show your answer and ALL your work clearly.

_____

_____

_____

_____

_____

_____

_____

_____

_____

_____

_____

_____

_____

_____

_____

_____

Name_____

Problem # _____ **, continued**

_____

_____

_____

_____

_____

_____

_____

_____

_____

_____

_____

_____

_____

_____

_____

_____

_____

_____

STOP

Fourth Grade Book of Math Tests

Geometry & Measurement
Skills Checklists

Geometry & Measurement Test # 1:

PLANE GEOMETRY

Test Location: pages 80–87

Skill	*Test Items*
Identify and describe points, lines, line segments, rays, and planes	1–6, 39
Identify different kinds of angles	7, 10
Identify and distinguish between parallel, perpendicular, and intersecting lines	8, 9, 11
Identify properties of a circle	13–15
Identify and define different polygons	15, 16, 20, 22, 25, 27, 29, 32, 34, 38, 40–42
Identify and define kinds of triangles	17–19, 37
Find the perimeter or circumference of plane figures	21, 23, 26, 28, 30, 33, 35
Choose correct formulas for finding area and perimeter of plane figures	21, 23, 24, 22, 24, 26, 28, 31, 32, 33, 35, 36
Distinguish among different quadrilaterals	22, 27, 32, 34, 43–46
Find the area of plane figures	24, 31, 36, 55–59
Recognize properties of different plane figures	37–42
Identify symmetrical figures	47
Identify congruent and similar figures	48–49
Recognize and draw transformations of plane figures	50–54
Solve word problems with geometric figures and concepts	55–60

Fourth Grade Book of Math Tests

SPACE GEOMETRY

Test Location: pages 88–91

Geometry & Measurement Test # 3

MEASUREMENT

Test Location: pages 92–99

                          Fourth Grade Book of Math Tests

PLANE GEOMETRY

Name _____   Possible Correct Answers: 60

Date _____   Your Correct Answers: _____

For problems 1-6, circle the correct answer.

---

1. XY is:
  A. a line segment D. a line
  B. a ray E. a point
  C. an angle F. a plane

4. FGH is:
  A. a line segment D. a line
  B. a ray E. a point
  C. an angle F. a plane

2. ST is:
  A. a line segment D. a line
  B. a ray E. a point
  C. an angle F. a plane

5. VW is:
  A. a line segment D. a line
  B. a ray E. a point
  C. an angle F. a plane

3. JKLM is:
  A. a line segment D. a line
  B. a ray E. a point
  C. an angle F. a plane

6. B is:
  A. a line segment D. a line
  B. a ray E. a point
  C. an angle F. a plane

80

Use the diagram for questions 7–11.
Circle the correct answer or answers for each question.
Some questions have more than one correct answer.

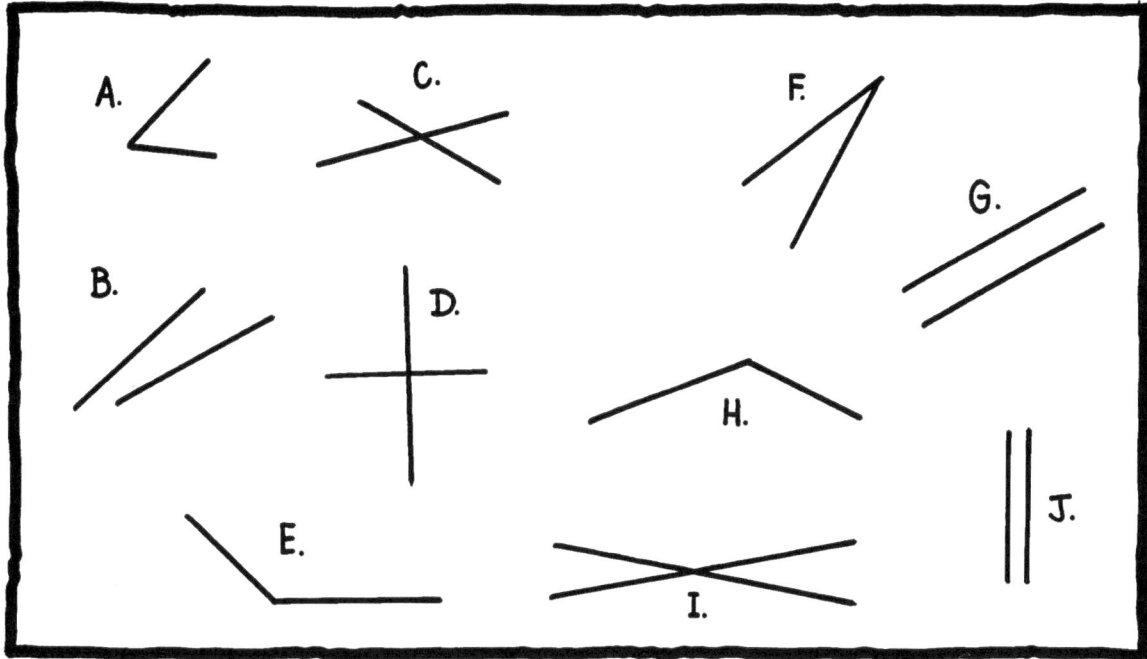

7. Which figures show obtuse angles?

    A   B   C   D   E

    F   G   H   I   J

8. Which figures show parallel lines?

    A   B   C   D   E

    F   G   H   I   J

9. Which figure shows perpendicular lines?

    A   B   C   D   E

    F   G   H   I   J

10. Which figures show acute angles?

    A   B   C   D   E

    F   G   H   I   J

11. Which figures show a pair of intersecting lines?

    A   B   C   D   E

    F   G   H   I   J

Name

Fourth Grade Book of Math Tests

12. Which line is a diameter? _____

13. Which line is a radius? _____

14. A gymnast warms up for her practice
   by jogging around the outside of a
   circular mat. The distance she is
   jogging is:
   - A. the diameter.
   - B. the circumference.
   - C. the radius.

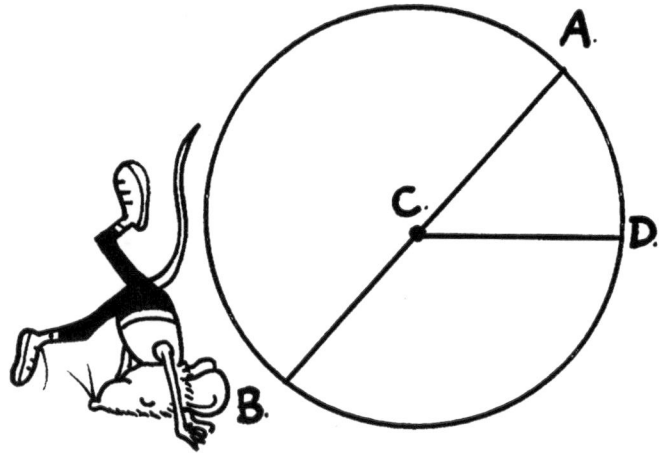

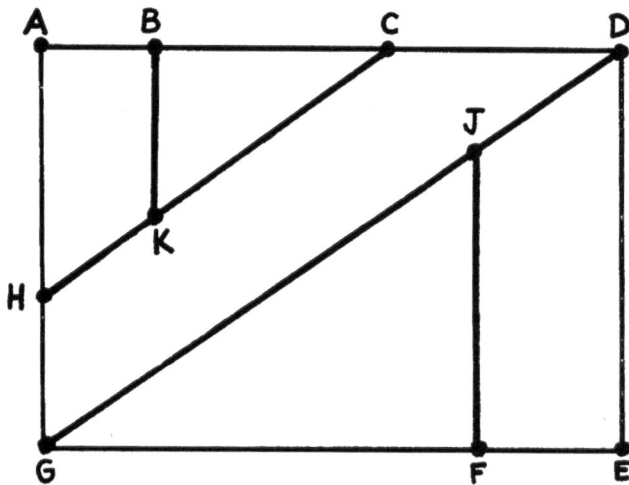

15. Which line divides the
   rectangle into two triangles? _____

16. Name four different triangles within
   this figure. Name each one by writing
   the three letters at its angles
   (example: XYZ).

   _____   _____

   _____   _____

17. Which flags are equilateral triangles?

   _____

18. Which flags are right triangles?

   _____

19. Which flags are isosceles triangles?

   _____

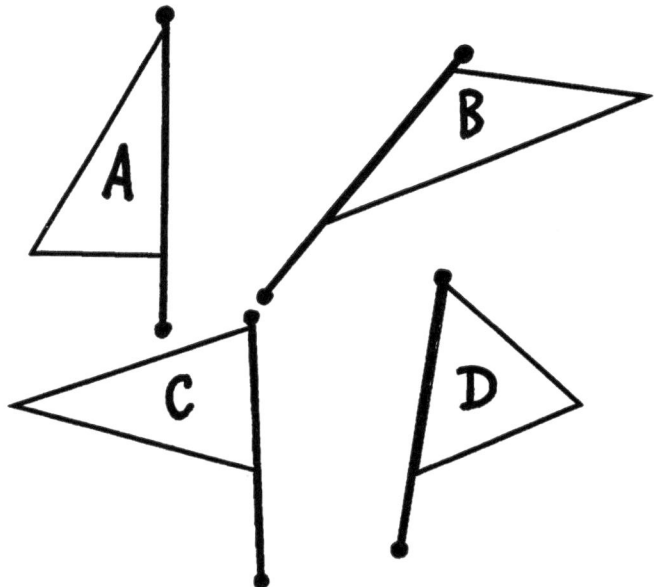

Name _____   **82**

Fourth Grade Book of Math Tests   Copyright ©2000 by Incentive Publications, Inc., Nashville, TN.

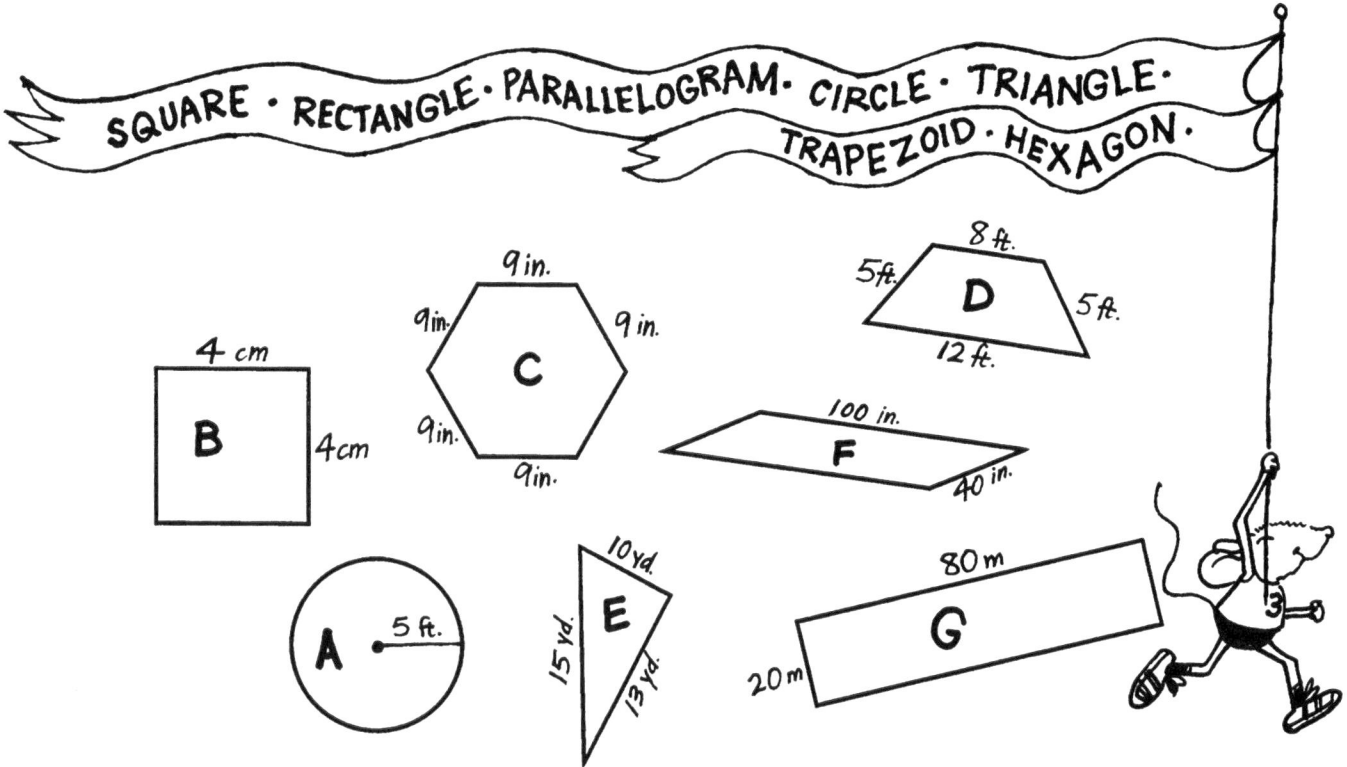

SQUARE · RECTANGLE · PARALLELOGRAM · CIRCLE · TRIANGLE · TRAPEZOID · HEXAGON ·

4 cm

B

4 cm

9 in.

9 in.   9 in.

C

9 in.   9 in.

9 in.

8 ft.

5 ft.   D   5 ft.

12 ft.

100 in.

F

40 in.

A   5 ft.

10 yd.

15 yd.   E   13 yd.

80 m

G

20 m

20. Figure A is a _____

21. The circumference of A is _____

22. Figure B is a _____

23. The perimeter of B is _____

24. The area of B is _____

25. Figure C is a _____

26. The perimeter of C is _____

27. Figure D is a _____

28. The perimeter of D is _____

29. Figure E is a _____

30. The perimeter of E is _____

31. The area of E is _____

32. Figure F is a _____

33. The perimeter of F is _____

34. Figure G is a _____

35. The perimeter of G is _____

36. The area of G is _____

Name _____

83

Fourth Grade Book of Math Tests

For questions 37–42, circle the correct answer.

37. The track team flag is a triangle with 2 sides equal. This triangle is:
    A. acute   C. equilateral
    B. scalene   D. isosceles

38. Elmo's gym bag has a 6–sided figure on it. This figure is a:
    A. quadrilateral   D. pentagon
    B. square   E. octagon
    C. hexagon

39. The first aid sign at the gym has two lines that cross each other at right angles. These lines are:
    A. parallel   B. perpendicular   C. Neither A or B

40. The award Rufus won is in a frame that is a quadrilateral. This frame has:
    A. four sides   B. three sides   C. six sides   D. five sides

41. The team symbol is a pentagon with flames around it. This pentagon has:
    A. four angles   B. no angles   C. five angles   D. three angles

42. The area at the track where the high jumpers practice is a shape that has four right angles. This shape of this area is:
    A. a triangle   B. a rectangle   C. a trapezoid   D. a hexagon

For questions 43–46, write **T** for true or **F** for false.

_____ 43. A square is a rectangle.

_____ 44. Trapezoids have 4 right angles.

_____ 45. A rectangle has 4 right angles.

_____ 46. A rectangle is a quadrilateral.

Fourth Grade Book of Math Tests   Copyright ©2000 by Incentive Publications, Inc., Nashville, TN.

47. Which figures are symmetrical?
    Circle the letters of the symmetrical figures.

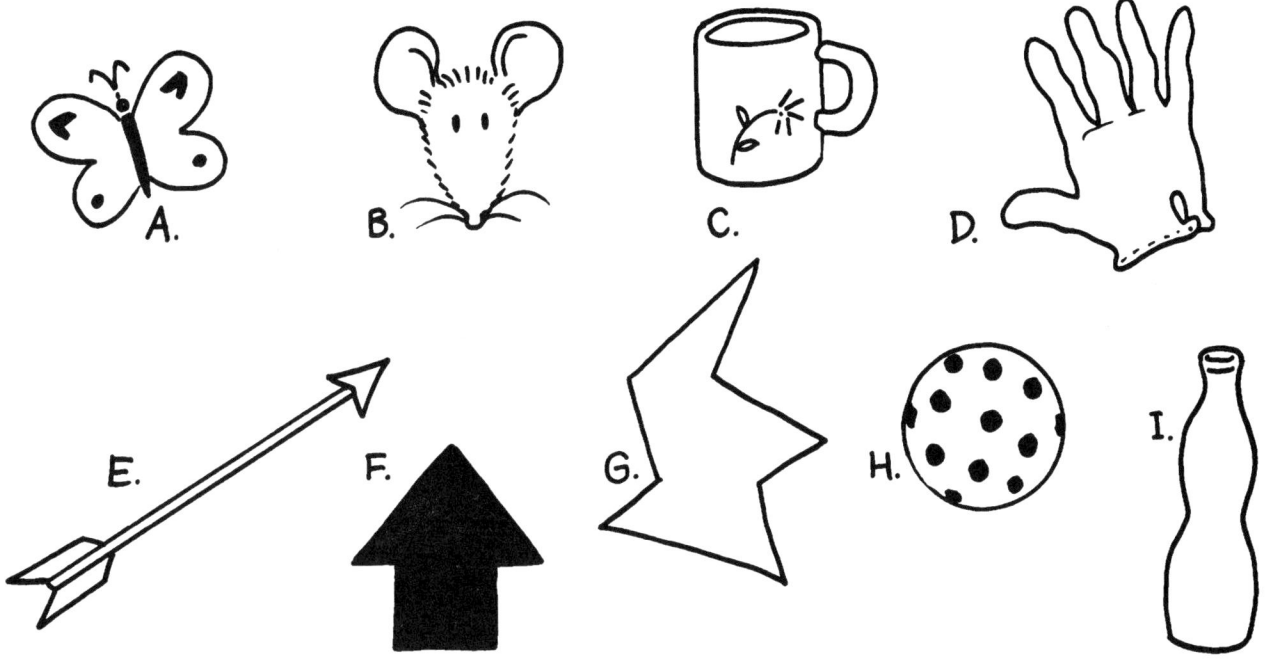

A.

B.

C.

D.

E.

F.

G.

H.

I.

48. Match the figures that are congruent to one another by drawing a line between them.

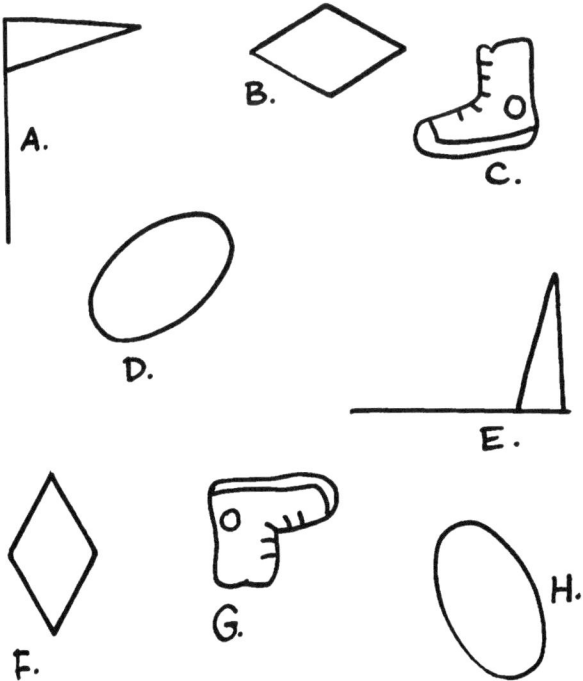

A.

B.

C.

D.

E.

F.

G.

H.

49. Match the figures that are similar to one another by drawing a line between them.

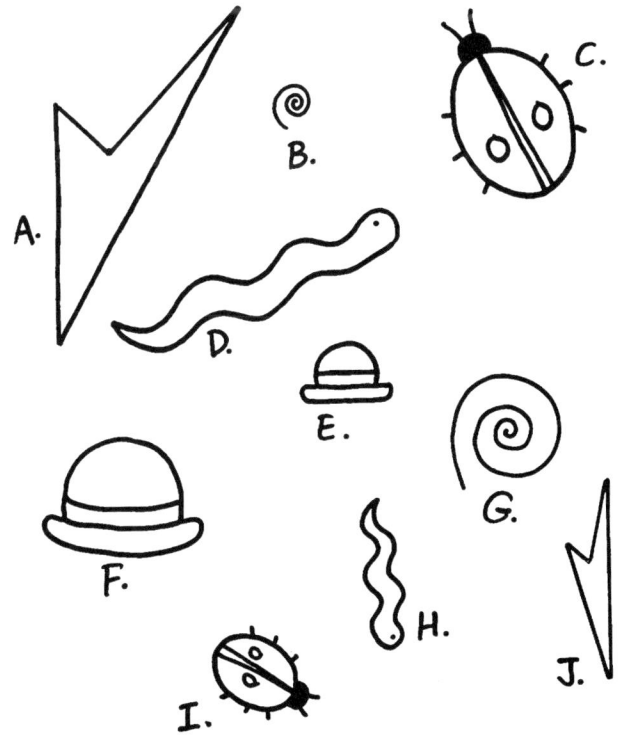

A.

B.

C.

D.

E.

F.

G.

H.

I.

J.

Name _____

85

50. Does this figure show a slide, flip, or turn? Circle one of the answers below.

slide

flip

turn

51. Does this figure show a slide, flip, or turn? Circle one of the answers below.

slide

flip

turn

52. Does this figure show a slide, flip, or turn? Circle one of the answers below.

slide

flip

turn

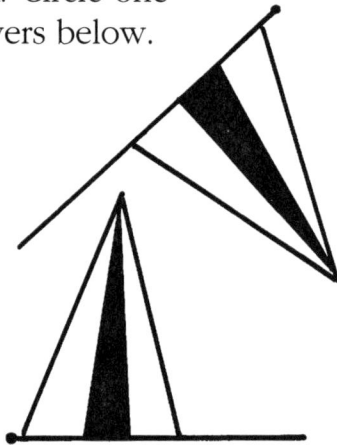

53. Draw a flip of this figure:

54. Draw a slide of this figure:

Name

86

55. The runners race on a circular track that has a radius of 50 feet. What formula should the runners use to find the area that the track surrounds? (Circle one answer.)

    A. $A = 2r^2$

    B. $A = \Pi r^2$

    C. $A = \Pi d$

    D. $A = r^2$

56. If the track has a radius of 50 feet, what is the area that it surrounds?

    A = _____

57. A cover has been made to protect the field during bad weather. The field is 100 yards long and 45 yards wide. What formula should be used to find the area that must be covered? (Circle one answer.)

    A. $A = s^2$

    B. $A = l^2 \times w^2$

    C. $A = l \times w$

    D. $A = 2(l + w)$

58. What is the area of the field described in the question above?

    A = _____

The swim team is collecting money to buy a cover for the pool. The cost of the cover is $ .50 a square foot. The swimmers must figure out the area of the pool surface, so they know how much money to collect. The pool is pictured below.

59. What is the surface area of the pool? _____

60. How much will the cover cost? _____

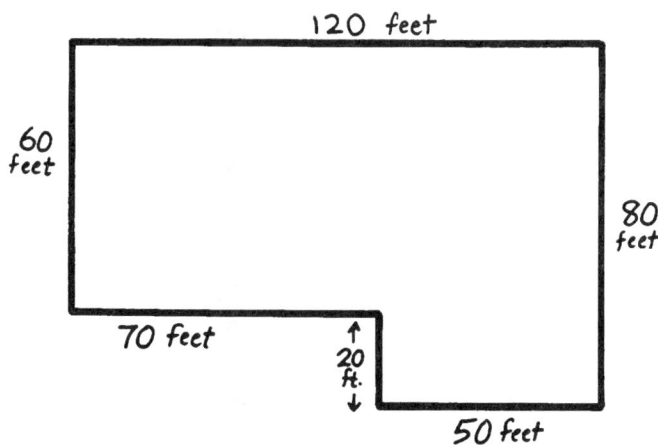

120 feet

60 feet

80 feet

70 feet

20 ft.

50 feet

STOP

Fourth Grade Book of Math Tests

SPACE GEOMETRY

Name _____

Possible Correct Answers: 25

Date _____

Your Correct Answers: _____

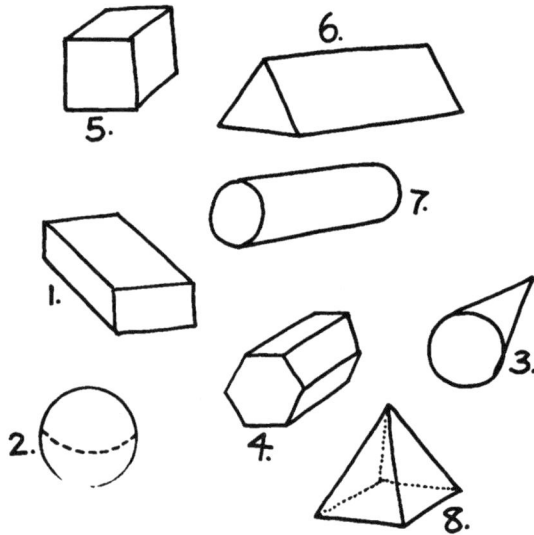

SPACE FIGURES
sphere
cube
cylinder
cone
pyramid
triangular prism
rectangular prism
hexagonal prism

Which figure is which?
Write the name of each space figure.

1. _____

2. _____

3. _____

4. _____

5. _____

6. _____

7. _____

8. _____

Fourth Grade Book of Math Tests

SPACE FIGURES

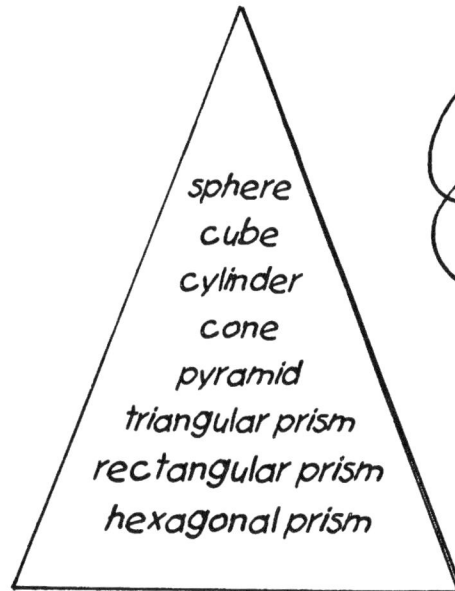

sphere
cube
cylinder
cone
pyramid
triangular prism
rectangular prism
hexagonal prism

Write the answer to each question.

9. Which space figure has two faces that are 6–sided? _____

10. Which space figure has two circular faces? _____

11. How many faces are on a cube? _____

12. How many edges are there on a sphere? _____

13. Which space figure has one circular face? _____

14. What is the shape of a pyramid's base? _____

15. What figure has two triangular bases? _____

16. How many faces are on a rectangular prism? _____

Name _____

Fourth Grade Book of Math Tests

1.

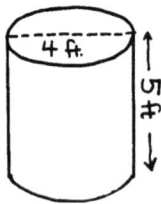

2.

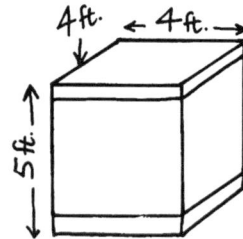

17. Which figure (above) has the greatest volume? _____

A

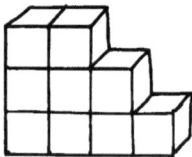

B

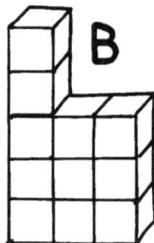

C

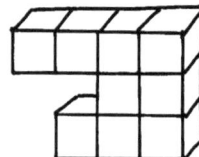

18. What is the volume of figure A (above)? _____ cubic units

19. What is the volume of figure B (above)? _____ cubic units

20. What is the volume of figure C (above)? _____ cubic units

21. What is the volume of this mat?

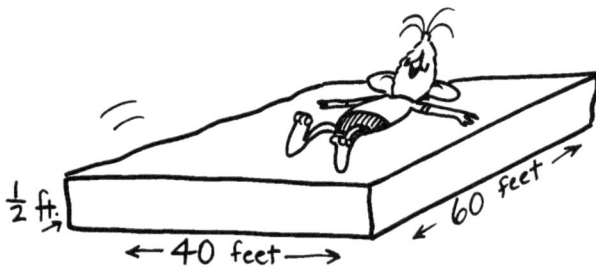

   A. 14,400 ft³

   B. 1,200 ft²

   C. 1,200 ft³

22. What is the volume of this mat?

   A. 1,600 in³

   B. 16,000 in³

   C. 160 in³

Name _____

Fourth Grade Book of Math Tests

Copyright ©2000 by Incentive Publications, Inc., Nashville, TN.

23. Which figure has a volume of about 100 cm³ ? _____

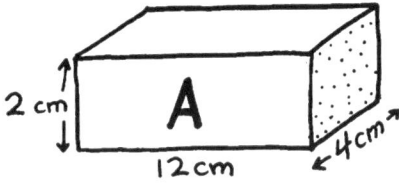 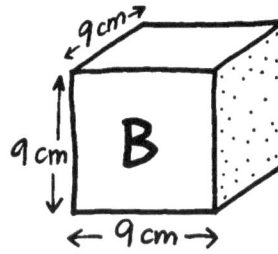

24. Which pool would hold about 50,000 ft³ of water? _____

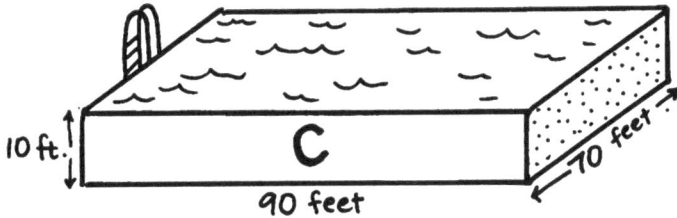 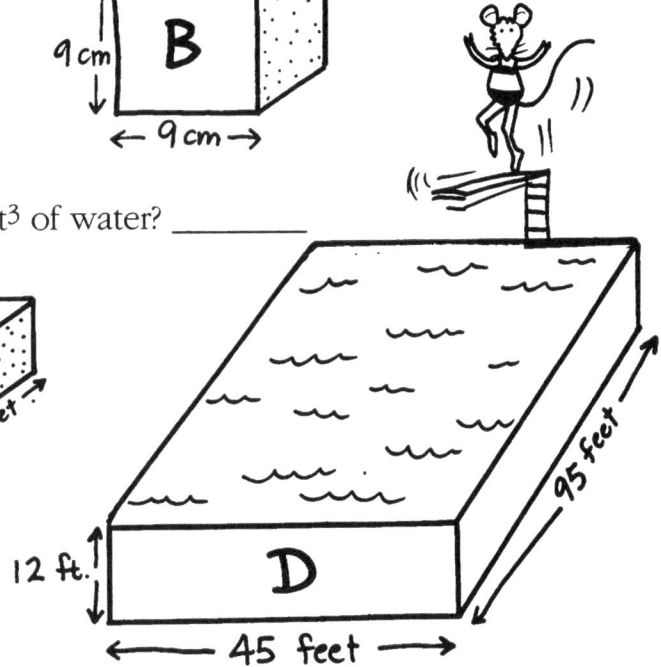

25. After the meet, the swimmers were offered two boxes full of good snacks. They had to choose one box. They wanted to choose the box that probably held the most snacks. Estimate the volume of both boxes to find out which one would hold the most.

These are the dimensions of the boxes:

Box # 1:   12 x 30 x 15 inches

Box # 2:   11 x 42 x 7 inches

Which box should they choose?

Answer: _____

Name _____

91

MEASUREMENT

Name _____   Possible Correct Answers: 75

Date _____   Your Correct Answers: _____

For items 1–16, tell what each unit measures.

1. kilogram

_____

2. meter

_____

3. liter

_____

4. foot

_____

5. mile

_____

6. inch

_____

7. kilometer

_____

8. gram

_____

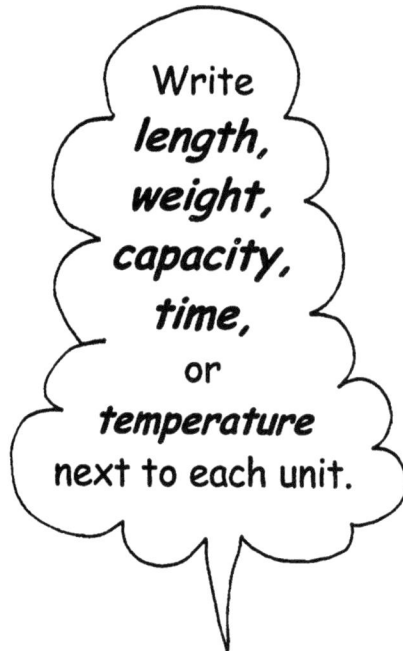

Write *length, weight, capacity, time,* or *temperature* next to each unit.

9. decade

_____

10. gallon

_____

11. centimeter

_____

12. ton

_____

13. quart

_____

14. yard

_____

15. degree

_____

16. century

_____

92

Circle the correct answer.

17. A gram is closest to

    A. a mile

    B. an ounce

    C. a pound

    D. a ton

    E. a mile

18. A mile is closest to

    A. a yard

    B. a week

    C. an acre

    D. a meter

    E. a kilometer

19. A liter is closest to

    A. a cup

    B. a pint

    C. a quart

    D. a tablespoon

    E. a gallon

20. An inch is closest to

    A. a yard

    B. a kilometer

    C. a meter

    D. a centimeter

    E. a milliliter

21. Which is the best estimate for the height of a rat?

    A. 2 centimeters

    B. 3 inches

    C. 4 meters

    D. 2 kilometers

22. Which is the best estimate for the weight of a golf club?

    A. 5 grams

    B. 10 milligrams

    C. 1 ounce

    D. 2 pounds

23. Which is the best estimate for the length of a boxing lesson?

    A. 1 hour

    B. 2 weeks

    C. 1 decade

    D. 20 seconds

24. Which is the best estimate for the capacity of a glass of sports drink?

    A. 3 liters

    B. 5 milliliters

    C. 3 gallons

    D. 2 cups

Name _____

93

Circle the correct answer.

25. Which measurement is most reasonable?
    A. the length of a boxing glove: 1.5 meters
    B. the amount of liquid in a milkshake: 18 ounces
    C. the weight of a hockey stick: 60 kilograms
    D. the distance from Chicago to Miami: 177 yards
    E. the temperature of a warm day: 290°

26. Which object would be about 25 centimeters in diameter?
    A. a ping pong ball
    B. an orange
    C. a ring for exercising horses
    D. a bowling ball
    E. a softball

27. Which could be measured in meters?
    A. the weight of a wrestler
    B. the temperature of hot chocolate
    C. the amount of water in a cup
    D. the depth of a swimming pool
    E. the speed of a race car

28. Which could be measured in grams?
    A. the weight of a gold medal won in a dance contest
    B. the length of a football game
    C. the height of a balance beam
    D. the circumference of a basketball
    E. the space taken up by air in a beachball

29. Which unit is best for measuring the length of a dancer's shoe?
    A. meters
    B. feet
    C. centimeters
    D. yards

30. Which unit is best for measuring the weight of a tennis ball?
    A. pounds
    B. tons
    C. kilograms
    D. ounces

31. Which unit is best for measuring the amount of air in an inflatable raft?
    A. cubic miles
    B. liters
    C. cubic inches
    D. gallons

Name _____

94

32. Which tool would be the best choice for measuring the time it takes to finish a game of golf?

    A. centimeter ruler

    B. a clock

    C. a scale

    D. a meter stick

34. Which tool would be the best choice for measuring the length of a tumbling mat?

    A. a meter stick

    B. a centimeter ruler

    C. a stop watch

    D. a thermometer

33. Which tool would be the best choice for measuring the amount of water a soccer team drinks during a game?

    A. a gallon container

    B. a cup

    C. a tablespoon

    D. a scale

35. Which tool would be the best choice for measuring the temperature of a weightlifter's shower?

    A. a clock

    B. a scale

    C. a thermometer

    D. a gallon container

For items 36–45, write ≤ (less than), ≥ (greater than), or = (equal to) in each blank.

36. 1 quart _____ 1 gallon

37. 1 gram _____ 1 kilogram

38. 6 months _____ 10 weeks

39. 1 hour _____ 80 minutes

40. 1 meter _____ 1 kilometer

41. 50 yards _____ 100 feet

42. 1 ton _____ 2000 pounds

43. 38 inches _____ 1 yard

44. 100 centimeters _____ 1 meter

45. 1 liter _____ 1 cup

Fourth Grade Book of Math Tests

These questions ask you to change one unit of measurement into another. Write the correct amount of the new measurement.

46. The travel time to a volleyball game was 6 hours. How many minutes? _____

47. A bag of snacks for the team weighs 1000 grams. How many kilograms? _____

48. The snow boarder fell down 10 yards from the finish line. How many feet? _____

49. A boxing match was over in 3 minutes. How many seconds? _____

50. Fans at the ski races drank 40 quarts of hot chocolate. How many gallons? _____

51. The swimmer was 100 centimeters from winning the race. How many meters? _____

52. A golf ball landed 144 inches from the hole. How many feet? _____

53. The bowling championship will be held in 9 weeks. How many days? _____

54. Rufus lifted a 6–pound weight. How many ounces? _____

55. It is 3 days until the next fencing lesson. How many hours? _____

56. Caspian has practiced archery every day for a year. How many days? _____

Fourth Grade Book of Math Tests Copyright ©2000 by Incentive Publications, Inc., Nashville, TN.

57. The bowling game starts in 4 hours and 20 minutes (from the time shown on the clock). What time does it start?

Answer: _____

58. The wrestling match ended $7\frac{1}{2}$ hours ago (from the time shown on the clock.). What time did it end?

Answer: _____

59. A weightlifting contest is scheduled to start at 2:00 p.m. this afternoon. The clock tells the time now. How much time do the weightlifters have left before the contest begins?

   A. $5\frac{1}{2}$ hours

   B. $6\frac{1}{2}$ hours

   C. 6 hours, 15 minutes

   D. 5 hours

60. The tickets to the fencing match were a bargain! They cost only 89¢. Which is NOT a way that a fan could pay for a ticket?
   A. 8 dimes, 9 pennies
   B. 3 quarters, 2 dimes, 1 nickel
   C. 2 quarters, 3 dimes, 9 pennies
   D. 17 nickels, 4 pennies

61. Which is NOT a way to make 45¢?
   A. 1 quarter, 2 dimes
   B. 1 quarter, 5 nickels
   C. 3 dimes, 15 pennies
   D. 9 nickels

62. Which is NOT a way to make 92¢?
   A. 6 dimes, 5 nickels, 6 pennies
   B. 3 quarters, 1 dime, 7 pennies
   C. 10 nickels, 42 pennies
   D. 8 dimes, 2 nickels, 2 pennies

63. Describe 2 different ways to make 55¢.

   _____

   _____

   _____

   _____

Name _____ **97** _____

Fourth Grade Book of Math Tests

64. Find the perimeter of this dance floor.

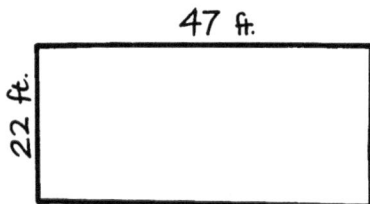

47 ft.

22 ft.

P = _____

65. Find the perimeter (circumference) of this boxing ring.

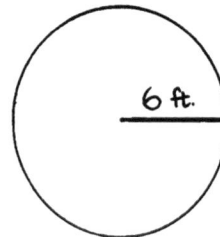

6 ft.

P = _____

66. Find the area of the sail on this sailboat.

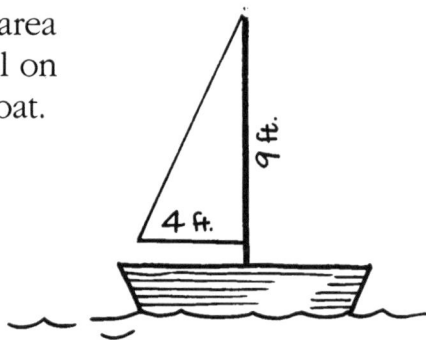

9 ft.

4 ft.

A = _____

67. Find the area of this mat.

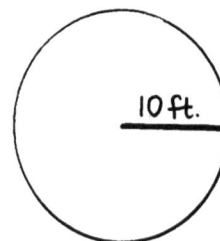

10 ft.

A = _____

68. A fisherman rows around the outside edge of a lake that is 500 feet wide and 1200 feet long. How far does he row?_____

69. The lawnkeeper mows a ball field that is 100 yards long and 60 yards wide. How much area does she mow?_____

70. Gigi rakes the inside of the paddock where she exercises her horse. The paddock is a triangle with a base of 100 feet and a height of 140 feet. How much area does she rake?_____

Name _____

Fourth Grade Book of Math Tests

Copyright ©2000 by Incentive Publications, Inc., Nashville, TN.

71. Find the volume of the diving pool.

V = _____

16 ft.

16 ft.

16 ft.

74. On Georgia's map of the bike trail, 1 inch represents $\frac{1}{2}$ mile of the trail. How much distance on the real trail is represented by 6 inches on Georgia's map?

_____

72. The floor of a storage closet at the gym measures by 6 feet by 7 feet. The ceiling in the closet is 8 feet high. What is the volume of the closet?

   A. 42 ft^2

   B. 48 ft^3

   C. 336 ft

   D. 336 ft^3

   E. 336 ft^2

75. Angelo's map of the archery course has a scale of 1 cm = 5 feet. How much distance at the course is represented by 8 cm?

_____

73. The weather on the day of the track meet caused runners to pay many visits to the sideline. There they rubbed ice on their necks, guzzled cold water, and wiped their heads, necks, and shoulders with dry towels. The temperature was probably about:

   A. 60° F

   B. 50° F

   C. 90° F

   D. 40° F

Name _____

Graphing, Statistics, & Probability
Skills Lists

Graphing, Statistics, & Probability Test # 1

COORDINATE GRAPHING

Test Location: pages 102–107

Graphing, Statistics, & Probability Test # 2

PROBABILITY

Test Location: pages 108–111

Fourth Grade Book of Math Tests

Graphing, Statistics, & Probability Test # 3

STATISTICS

Test Location: pages 112–115

Graphing, Statistics, & Probability Test # 4

STATISTICS & GRAPHS

Test Location: pages 116–120

Fourth Grade Book of Math Tests

COORDINATE GRAPHING

Name _____

Possible Correct Answers: 55

Date _____

Your Correct Answers: _____

In a shoe-tossing contest, shoes have landed all over the grid.

Shoe-Tossing Contest

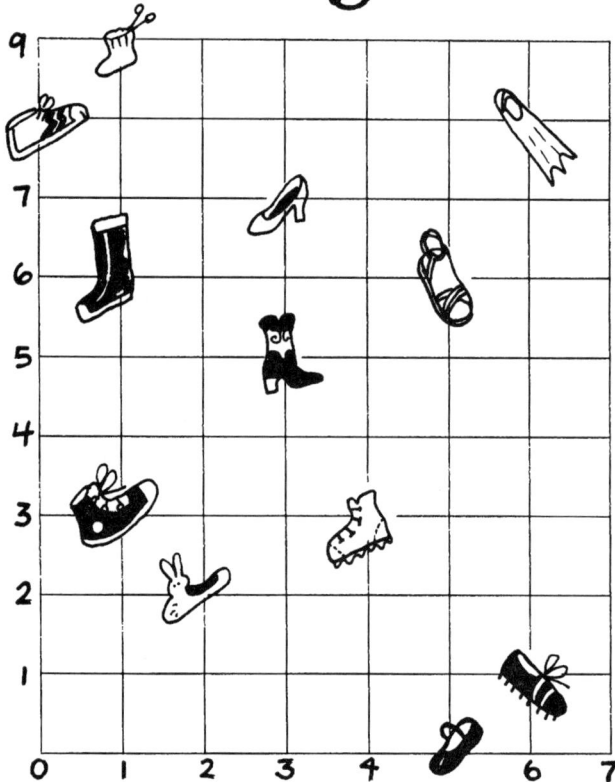

Draw or describe the shoe found at each of these locations:

1. (1, 9) _____

2. (0, 8) _____

3. (1, 3) _____

4. (3, 5) _____

Write the coordinate location of each of these. Write coordinates like this: (4, 3).

_____ 5. hiking boot

_____ 6. baby bootie

_____ 7. bunny slipper

_____ 8. sandal

_____ 9. swim fin

_____ 10. cowboy boot

_____ 11. high-heeled shoe

_____ 12. soccer shoe

102

Follow the instructions to finish putting worms on the grid for the great worm race.

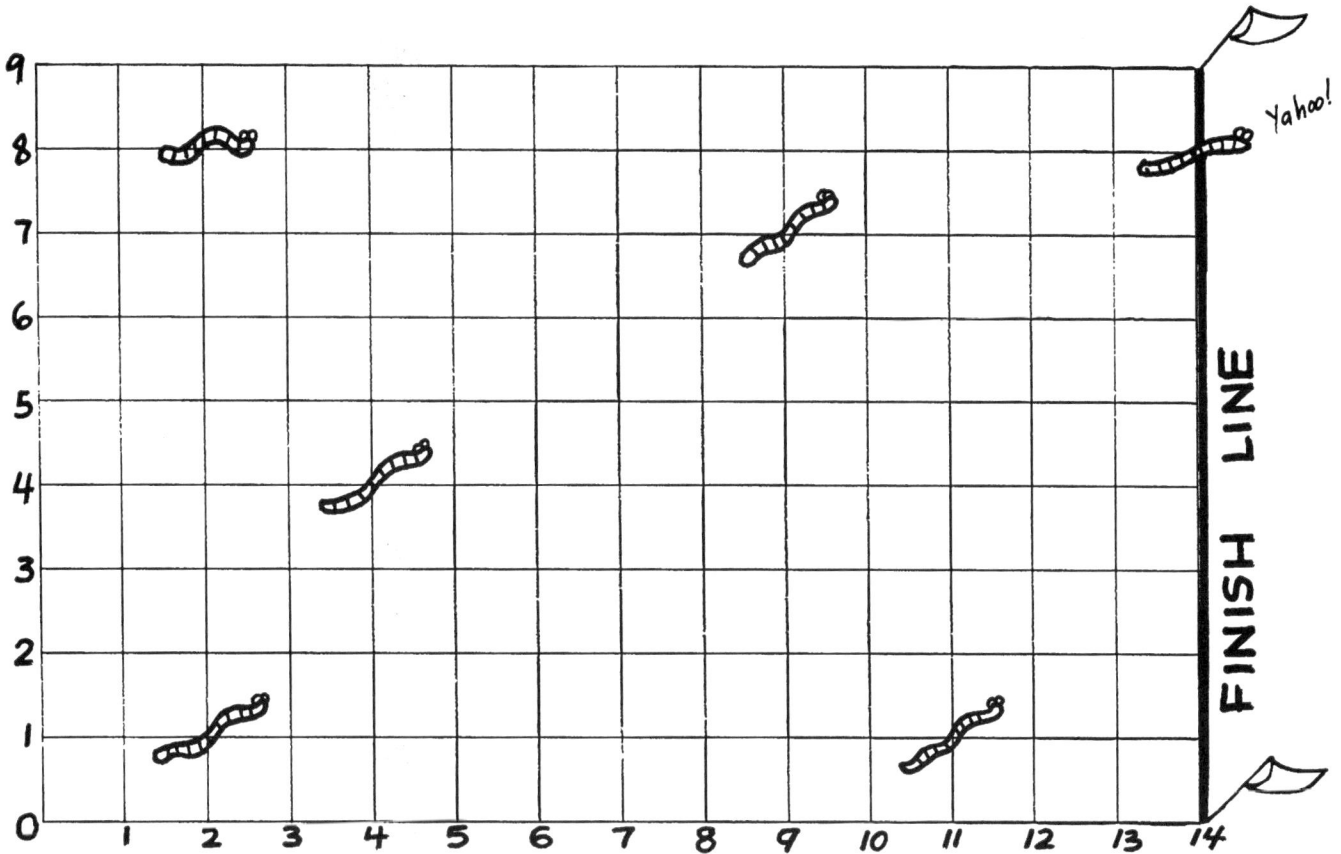

Yahoo!

FINISH LINE

WORM RACES
TODAY

13. What worm is at the finish line? Write its location (coordinates).

_____

14. Write the location (coordinates) of the five other worms shown:

_____

_____

_____

_____

_____

15. Draw a worm at (7, 0).

16. Draw a worm at (10, 4).

17. Draw a worm at (8, 3).

18. Draw a worm at (0, 5).

19. Draw a worm at (13, 9).

20. Draw a worm at (8, 9).

21. Draw a worm at (2, 3).

22. Draw a worm that stretches from (6, 6) to (8, 7).

Name

Fourth Grade Book of Math Tests

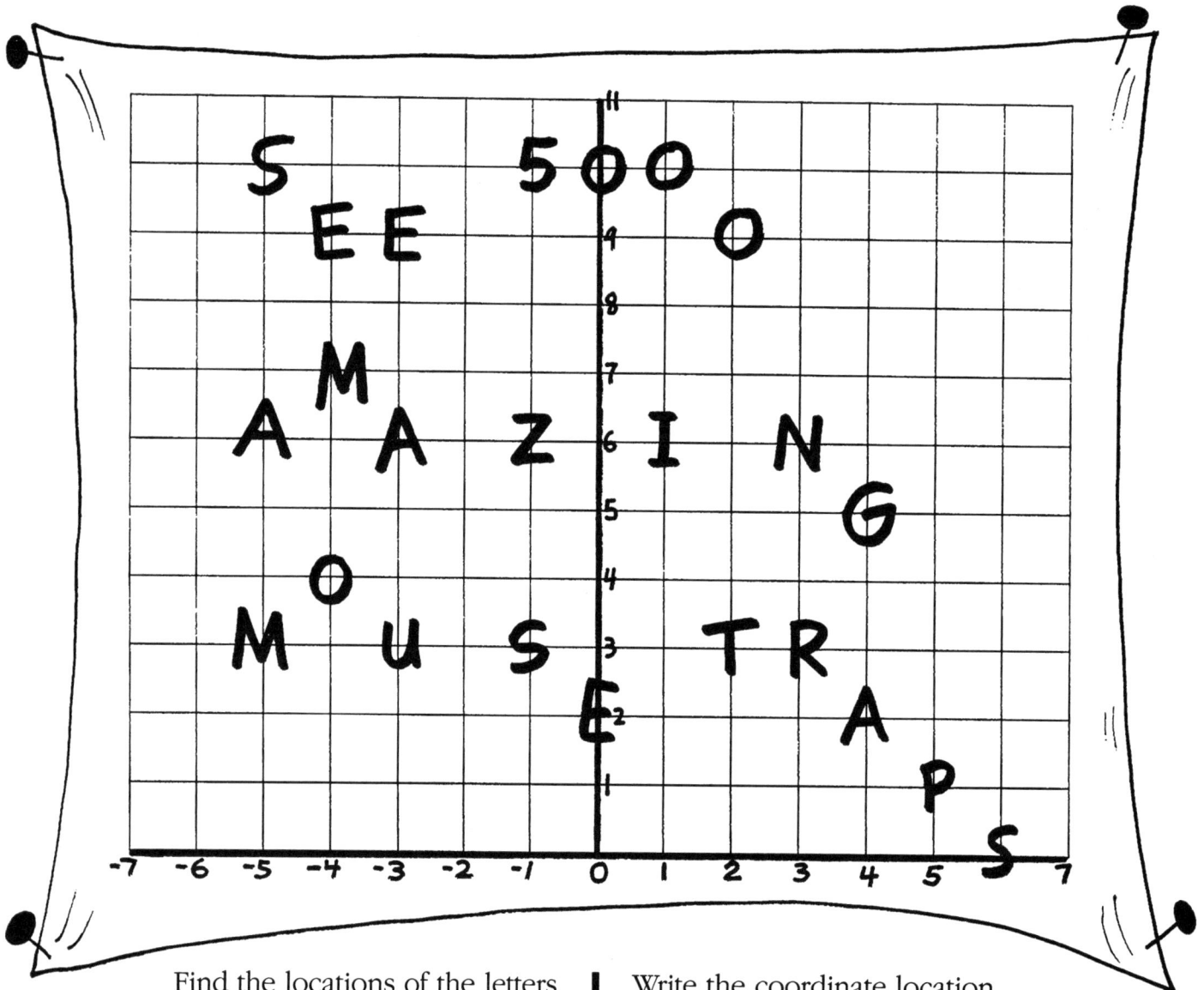

Find the locations of the letters or numbers on the poster grid.

23. What is located at (3, 6)? _____

24. What is located at (–3, 3)? _____

25. What is located at (–4, 7)? _____

26. What is located at (0, 10)? _____

27. What is located at (5, 1)? _____

Write the coordinate location of each of these letters or numbers.

_____ 28. All Es

_____ 29. G

_____ 30. 5

_____ 31. T

_____ 32. All As

Name _____

— 104 —

Many records have been set with collections. When you finish these problems, the grid will hold pictures of some of the things that make up famous collections.

Draw these items at the coordinate locations shown.

33. Draw a marble at (3, 0).

34. Draw a light bulb at (−4, 5).

35. Draw a magnet at (4, 9).

36. Draw a watch at (−6, 7).

37. Draw a piggy bank at (−6, 0).

38. Draw a teddy bear at (2, 7).

39. Draw a bubble at (−2, 2).

40. Draw a golf ball at (0, 5).

41. Draw a garbage can at (6, 1).

42. Draw a shoe at (−5, 8).

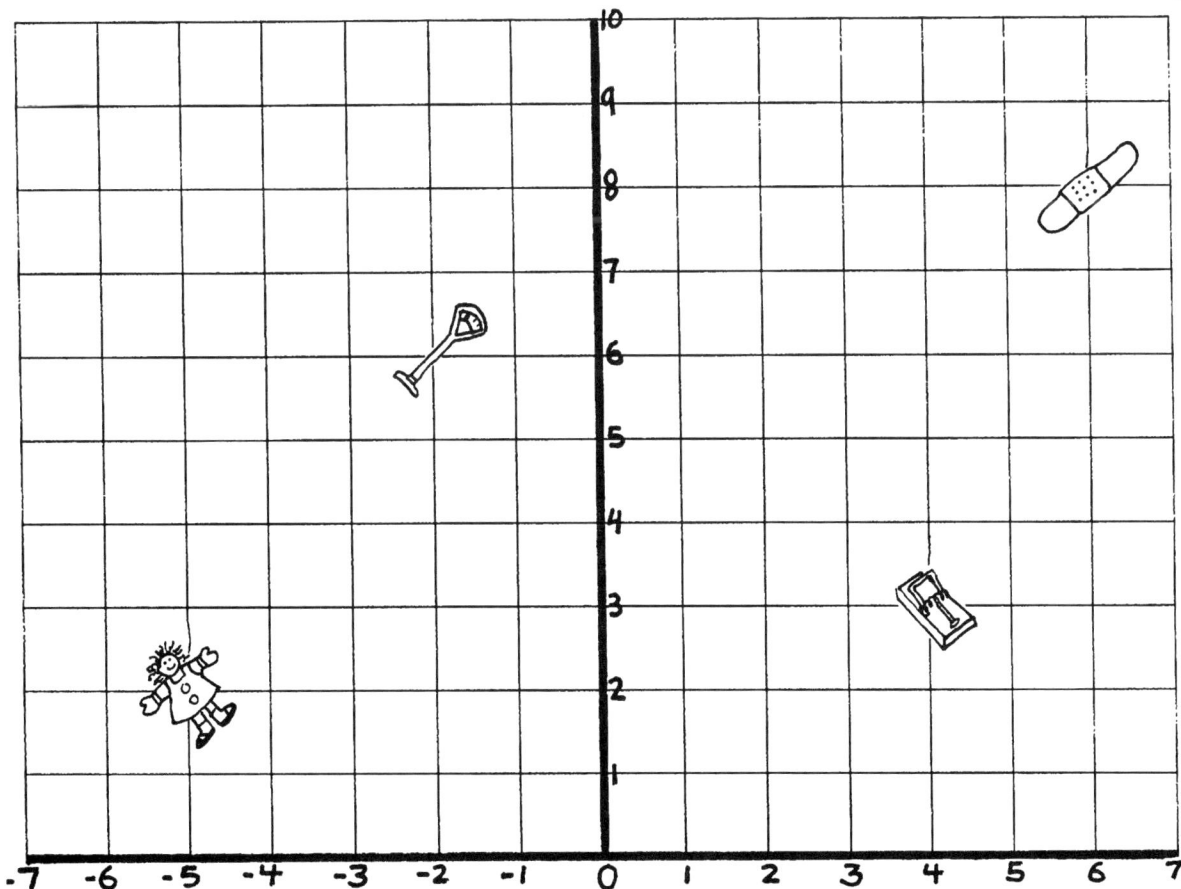

Fourth Grade Book of Math Tests

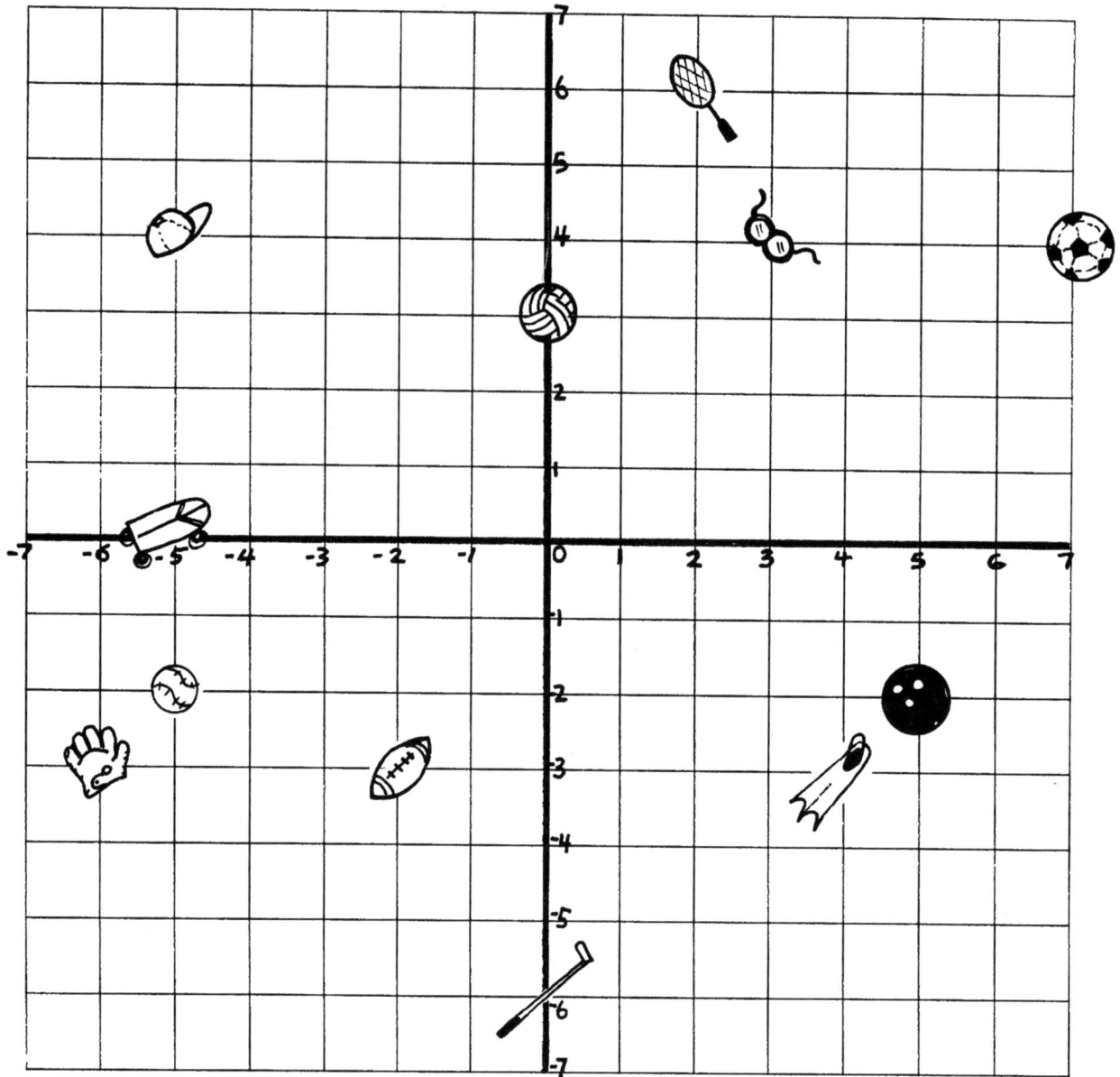

What is found at these locations? Draw or describe the sports item.

43. (4, −3) _____

44. (0, 3) _____

45. (3, 4) _____

46. (−2, −3) _____

47. (5, −2) _____

48. (−5, 0) _____

Write the coordinates of these items. Write coordinates like this: (3, 2).

49. baseball mitt _____

50. tennis racquet _____

51. golf club _____

52. baseball _____

53. baseball cap _____

54. soccer ball _____

Name _____

106

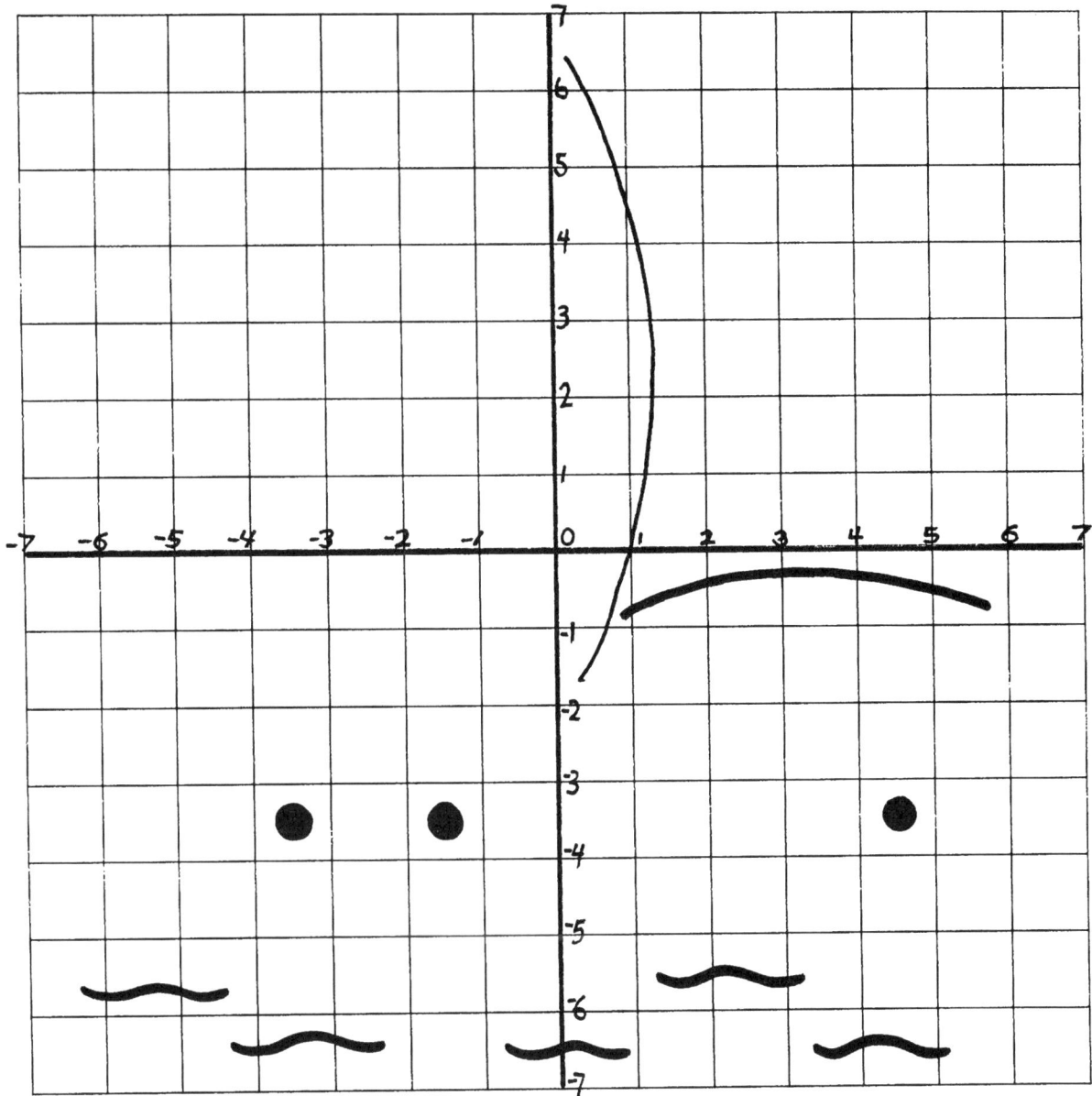

Follow the directions to find something that provides many thrills for adventuresome racers.

Draw a fat point at each of these locations. Then connect them with a line that touches each point, in order.

(0, –3); (–1, –3); (–2, –2);
(–6, –2); (–4, –5); (0, –5);
(5, –5); (6, –3); (0, –3)

Now, draw a point at each of these locations. Then connect the points in order.

(0, –2);
(7, –2);
(5, 2);
(2, 5);
(0, 7)

Name _____

Fourth Grade Book of Math Tests

PROBABILITY

Name _____

Possible Correct Answers: 30

Date _____

Your Correct Answers: _____

1. Racers at the stilt-racing contest race against the clock. A coin is tossed to see which team gets to race first. What is likely to happen?

    A. It is most likely that the coin will land with heads up.

    B. It is most likely that the coin will land with tails up.

    C. Heads and tails are equally likely.

2. One rider from each state in the USA is taking part in a motorcycle race. One racer's name is chosen from a hat. How likely is it that this rider is from Oklahoma?

    A. 1 out of 49 (1/49)

    B. 1 out of 50 (1/50)

    C. 50 out of 1 (50/1)

    D. 49 out of 1 (49/1)

3. A group that is planning the big bed-racing contest is trying to choose a month to hold the competition. They decide to put the names of all the months in a hat and draw one. Which is the most likely outcome?

    A. The month will begin with the letter M.

    B. The month will begin with the letter A.

    C. The month will begin with the letter J.

    D. All months are equally likely.

4. Rufus is having a great time at the balloon-bursting contest. After he is blindfolded, he has 10 seconds to burst as many balloons as he can. His group of balloons contains:

    13 purple
    18 red
    7 white
    9 green

    Which color is he most likely to hit first?

    A. white

    B. red

    C. purple

    D. green

5. Two coins are flipped. What are all the possible ways the coins can land? Write the possible outcomes. Use H for heads and T for tails.

    _____

    _____

108

Caspian is ready to take his turn at the Dairy County Milkshake-Drinking Contest. Before he starts, he must spin the spinner to pick the kind of milkshake he will drink.

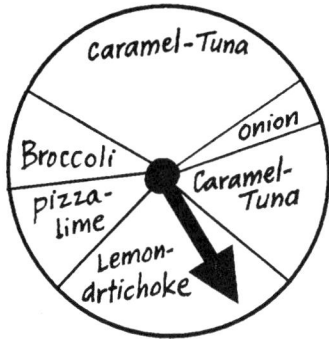

6. How many different outcomes are possible?

_____

7. Which is the most likely flavor?

_____

8. Which flavor is least likely?

_____

9. Which flavors are equally likely?

_____

10. The leapfrog contest begins with a toss of dice to decide which pair of leapers goes first. If ONE die is tossed, what is the probability that it will land with a "4" showing?
    A. 1/6
    B. 6/1
    C. 1/4
    D. 1/4
    E. None of these

Two coins are tossed at the same time.

11. What is the probability that the outcome will be 2 heads?

_____

12. What is the probability that the outcome will NOT be 2 tails?

_____

At the Big Bubble Sculpture Competition, wonderful creations are built out of bubbles. The bubble builders must work fast—before the bubbles break!
Builders work in pairs. Four friends came to the contest together: Gracie, Ellie, Abby, and Millie.

13. What are all the possible pairs that these four friends could form? Write them:

_____

_____

_____

_____

Fourth Grade Book of Math Tests

Leo is in a hurry to get to the dance contest. He has forgotten his shoes!
The picture shows the numbers and colors of his shoes in the closet.
Quickly, Leo reaches into his dark closet and grabs a shoe.

14. What is the probability
    that the shoe will be blue? _____

15. What is the probability
    that the shoe will be red? _____

16. What is the probability that
    the shoe will NOT be black? _____

17. What is the probability that
    the shoe will be red or black? _____

6 red shoes

2 blue shoes

4 green shoes

8 black shoes

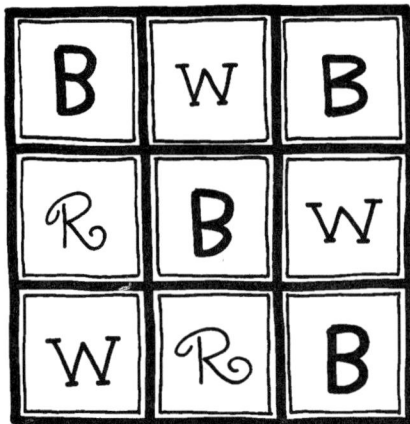

Reggie has made it all the way to the finals in a
dart-throwing contest. He throws his first dart.

18. What is the probability that
    the dart will hit a blue square? _____

19. What is the probability that
    the dart will hit a white square? _____

20. What is the probability that
    the dart will hit a square
    that is NOT red? _____

Georgia has gotten very good at balancing eggs on a
plate. There are 5 pink eggs, 7 yellow eggs, 2 blue eggs,
and 4 green eggs. Ooops! One egg falls off and breaks!
What is the probability that . . .

21. the broken egg is NOT green? _____

22. the broken egg is yellow? _____

23. the broken egg is pink? _____

24. the broken egg is pink or yellow? _____

Name _____

Fourth Grade Book of Math Tests

In a very unusual contest, competitors try to lift very heavy objects!
At the contest, the names of objects to be lifted are placed in a hat. Each competitor
draws a card. Then he or she must try to lift the object named on the card.

These are the cards in the hat. Angelo draws a card.

25. What is the probability that
    Angelo will be lifting a panther or an elephant? _____

26. What is the probability that
    Angelo will be lifting a bus or an ostrich? _____

27. What is the probability that
    Angelo will be lifting an animal? _____

28. What is the probability that
    Angelo will be lifting a vehicle? _____

29. What is the probability that
    Angelo will be lifting a train? _____

30. Which item is Angelo most likely to pick? _____

Name _____ **111** _____

STATISTICS

Name _____   Possible Correct Answers: 30

Date _____   Your Correct Answers: _____

Choose the matching term for each definition.
Write the letter on the line.

_____ 1. information given in number form

_____ 2. the average of a number of data items

_____ 3. a graph that uses lines to show
changes in data over time

_____ 4. the number of times an item appears
in a set of data

_____ 5. a graph that uses pictures or symbols
to stand for numbers or amounts

_____ 6. the least and greatest numbers in a
set of data

A. frequency

B. line graph

C. statistics

D. data

E. bar graph

F. mean

G. circle graph

H. pictograph

I. range

Use the Cheese-Eating Record chart for
questions 7–8.

7. What is the mean (average) number of
pounds of cheese eaten by each rat?

_____

8. What is the range of the amounts of
cheese eaten by the rats?

_____

Cheese-Eating Records

RAT	Number of Pounds eaten in one day
Elmo	11
Abby	8
Reggie	10
Georgio	9
Rufus	12

Fourth Grade Book of Math Tests

Use this frequency tally sheet for questions 9–12.

9. What age group had the most onion eaters?

_____

10. What was the total number of onion eaters ages 11–15?

_____

11. How many onion eaters were over 30?

_____

12. Were there more onion eaters ages 16–30 or ages 31–50?

_____

ONION EATER'S CONTEST
Ages of Contestants

Ages	Tally	Total Number
5-10	ⅢⅢ |||	8
11-15	ⅢⅢ ⅢⅢ ⅢⅢ ⅢⅢ		
16-20	ⅢⅢ ⅢⅢ ⅢⅢ		16
21-30	ⅢⅢ ⅢⅢ ⅢⅢ |||	18
31-40	ⅢⅢ ⅢⅢ ||	
41-50	ⅢⅢ ||	7
over 50	ⅢⅢ ||||	

Use the **Frequency of Dropouts** table for questions 13–16.

13. How many more adults than children dropped out of the contest on Saturday?

_____

14. Overall, did more children or more adults drop out of the contests?

_____

15. Which day had the most dropouts?

_____

16. How many days had fewer dropouts than Tuesday?

_____

Frequency of Drop-Outs
from the Onion Eating Contest

Contest Day	Number of Adults	Number of Children
Monday	18	6
Tuesday	11	8
Wednesday	3	0
Thursday	14	2
Friday	5	11
Saturday	23	9

Yuck!

Name _____

Fourth Grade Book of Math Tests

Use the ***How Big Was It?*** table for questions 17–20.

HOW BIG WAS IT?
Record-Breaking Sizes

ITEM	SIZE
Biggest pizza	122- foot diameter
Biggest chocolate pie	78-foot diameter
Longest sandwich	2 miles
Largest Stocking	38 feet long
Longest salami	68 feet
Biggest ice cube	1000 square feet
Tallest sand castle	21 feet
Biggest pickle	87 inches long
Heaviest pumpkin	954 pounds
Tallest dandelion	29 inches
Biggest jawbreaker	11-inch diameter

17. Which is greater, the diameter of the chocolate pie or the length of the stocking?

_____

18. How much longer than the dandelion is the pickle?

_____

19. If the salami were stood on its end next to the sandcastle, how much higher would it stand than the sandcastle?

_____

20. How much smaller is the chocolate pie than the pizza?

_____

Use the ***How Long Did It Take to Eat That?*** table for questions 21–24.

HOW LONG DID IT TAKE TO EAT THAT?
Record-Setting Times

Food	Amount	Time it Took to Set the Record
raw eggs	13	1 second
cooked eggs	14	14 seconds
bananas	17	2 minutes
sausage	6 pounds	3 minutes, 10 seconds
lemons (peels included)	3	15 seconds
hot dogs	30	64 seconds
spaghetti	100 yards	12 seconds

21. Which food took about as long to eat as the time it took to eat the lemons? _____

22. How much longer did it take to eat the sausage than the bananas? _____

23. Which took 63 seconds less time to eat than the hot dogs? _____

24. Which two records, completed one after the other, would take 26 seconds?

_____ and _____

Name _____

Fourth Grade Book of Math Tests
Copyright ©2000 by Incentive Publications, Inc., Nashville, TN.

Use the **Spitting Contest** table for questions 25–30.

SPITTING CONTEST
Record-Setting Distances in inches

Item	Winnie	Minnie	Vinnie	Lennie
Watermelon Seeds	42	33	46	30
Crickets	23	29	13	19
Peanuts	50	52	44	41
Cherry Pits	18	20	48	32
Peach Pits	10	13	11	9
Popcorn Kernels	20	44	45	46

25. Which item seems to be the most difficult to spit a long distance? _____

26. Who spit a cherry pit the farthest? _____

27. How much farther was Minnie's peanut record than her peach pit record?

_____

28. What was the difference between the greatest and the least cricket-spitting distance?

_____

29. What is the range of the distances for watermelon seed spitting distances?

_____

30. Did anyone have the best record for more than one item? _____ If so, who was it?

_____

Name _____ 115 _____

STATISTICS & GRAPHS

Name _____ Possible Correct Answers: 35

Date _____ Your Correct Answers: _____

Eeeek

SNAKE SITTING RECORDS

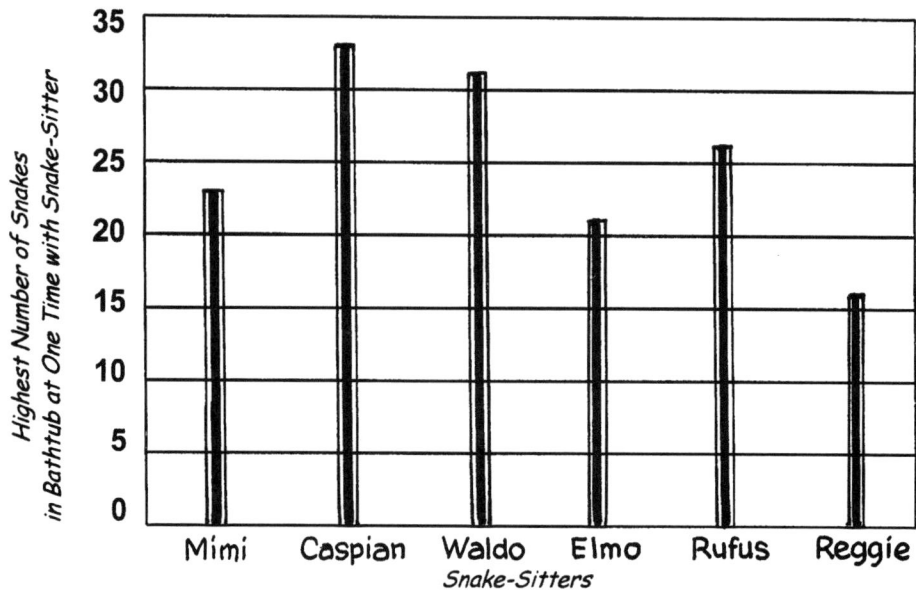

Highest Number of Snakes in Bathtub at One Time with Snake-Sitter

35		
30		
25		
20		
15		
10		
5		
0		

Mimi   Caspian   Waldo   Elmo   Rufus   Reggie

Snake-Sitters

1. How many snake-sitters have a better record than Elmo? _____

2. Whose record is about 10 more snakes than Reggie's? _____

3. Who sat in a tub with 31 snakes? _____

4. Who sat in a tub with 23 snakes? _____

5. About how many snakes were in the tub with Caspian? _____

6. Whose record is about 3 snakes more than Mimi's? _____

Rufus is a champion bubble blower. He's trying to improve and blow bigger bubbles in time for his next contest. The graph shows his progress over ten weeks of practice.

PRACTICING FOR RECORD BREAKING BUBBLES

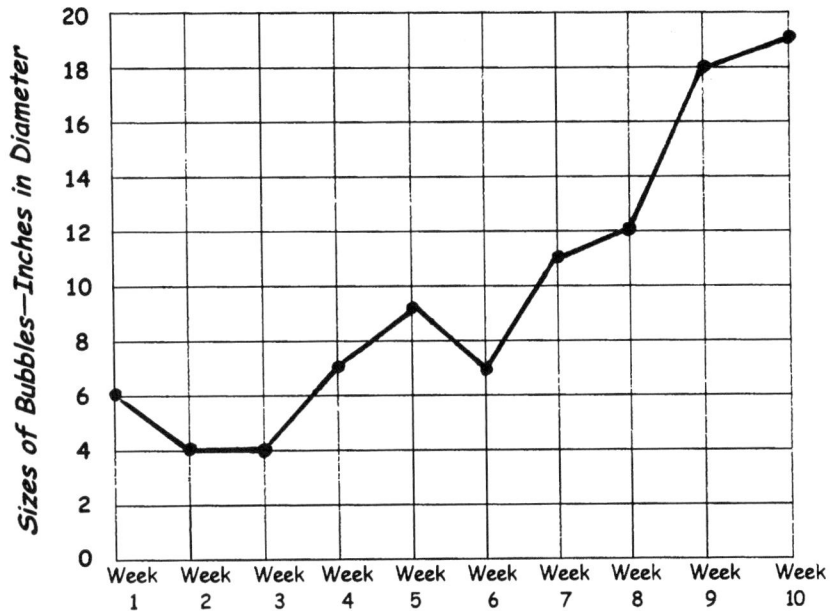

Sizes of Bubbles—Inches in Diameter

Week 1, Week 2, Week 3, Week 4, Week 5, Week 6, Week 7, Week 8, Week 9, Week 10

7. In which week is he able to blow 11–inch bubbles?

_____

8. How much bigger are his bubbles in week 10 than in week 1?

_____

9. In which three weeks did Rufus NOT improve over the previous week?

_____

10. Between which two weeks did Rufus make the most progress?

_____

The graph shows how Rufus spent the prize money he won in a bubble-blowing contest. Use the graph to answer the questions.

11. How much did Rufus spend on cheese curls? _____

12. How much did Rufus spend on pie and lasagna together?

_____

13. How much did Rufus spend on plain cheese? _____

14. What was the total prize? _____

HOW RUFUS SPENT HIS PRIZE MONEY

Cheese Curls $25.

Cheese lasagna $22.

Cheese Pie $25.

Cheese $4.

Cheese Pudding $24.

munch munch

Cheese Curls

Name _____

Fourth Grade Book of Math Tests

These friends are balancing light bulbs in an effort to break the record.
Use the graph to answer the questions about how they are doing.

RECORDS for BALANCING LIGHTBULBS

ANGIE	💡💡💡💡💡💡
MILLIE	💡💡💡💡💡💡💡💡💡
GINA	💡💡💡💡
GEORGIA	💡💡💡💡💡💡💡
WINNIE	💡💡💡💡💡💡💡

💡 = 5 light bulbs

15. How many light bulbs has Millie successfully balanced? _____

16. Who balanced about 28 bulbs? _____

17. How many competitors balanced more bulbs than Angie? _____

18. Who has balanced about 33 bulbs? _____

19. Who has balanced about 8 bulbs more than Angie? _____

20. Who has balanced more than twice as many as Gina? _____

21. How many bulbs has Winnie successfully balanced? _____

Name _____

Fourth Grade Book of Math Tests

Rufus and Caspian are trying to see how many pizza crusts they can toss into the air and catch without dropping. Use the graph to answer the questions about how they are doing.

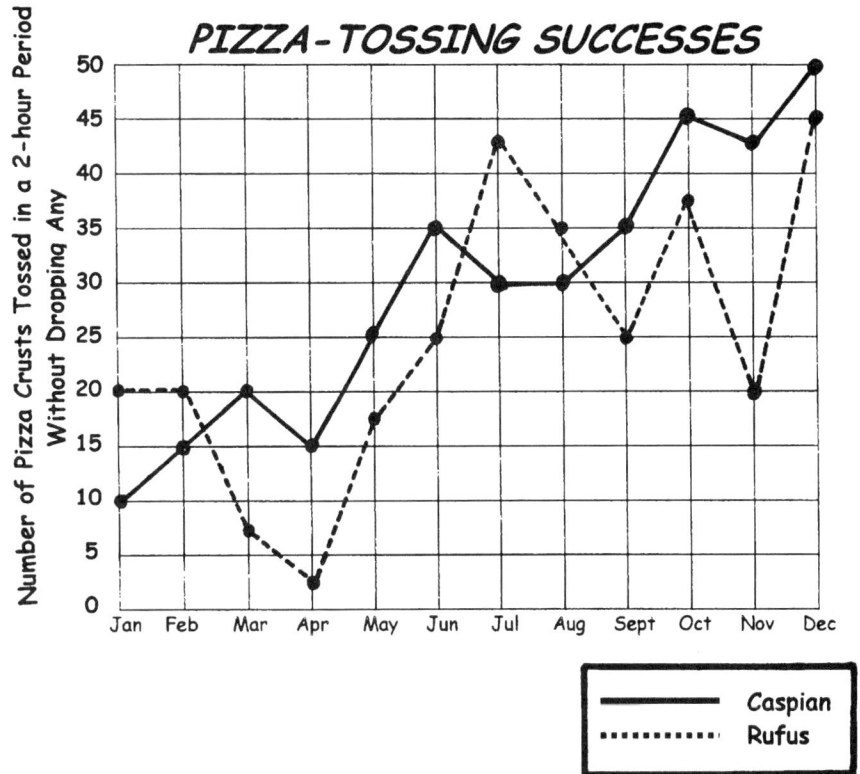

PIZZA-TOSSING SUCCESSES

Number of Pizza Crusts Tossed in a 2-hour Period Without Dropping Any

——— Caspian
··········· Rufus

22. In what month did Rufus successfully toss 42 pizza crusts? _____

23. What was the number of pizza-tossing successes in Caspian's worst month? _____

24. Whose December total was the most improved from his January total?

_____

25. Who tossed the most pizzas in July? _____

26. Were there any months in which both tossed the same number? _____

27. What was Rufus's best month? _____

28. In which two months did Caspian toss 30 pizza crusts? _____

Name _____

Fourth Grade Book of Math Tests

Use the graph to answer questions about the challenge between the two top roller-coaster riders. The graph shows the number of times each competitor rode five of the terrifying coasters over a period of 24 hours.

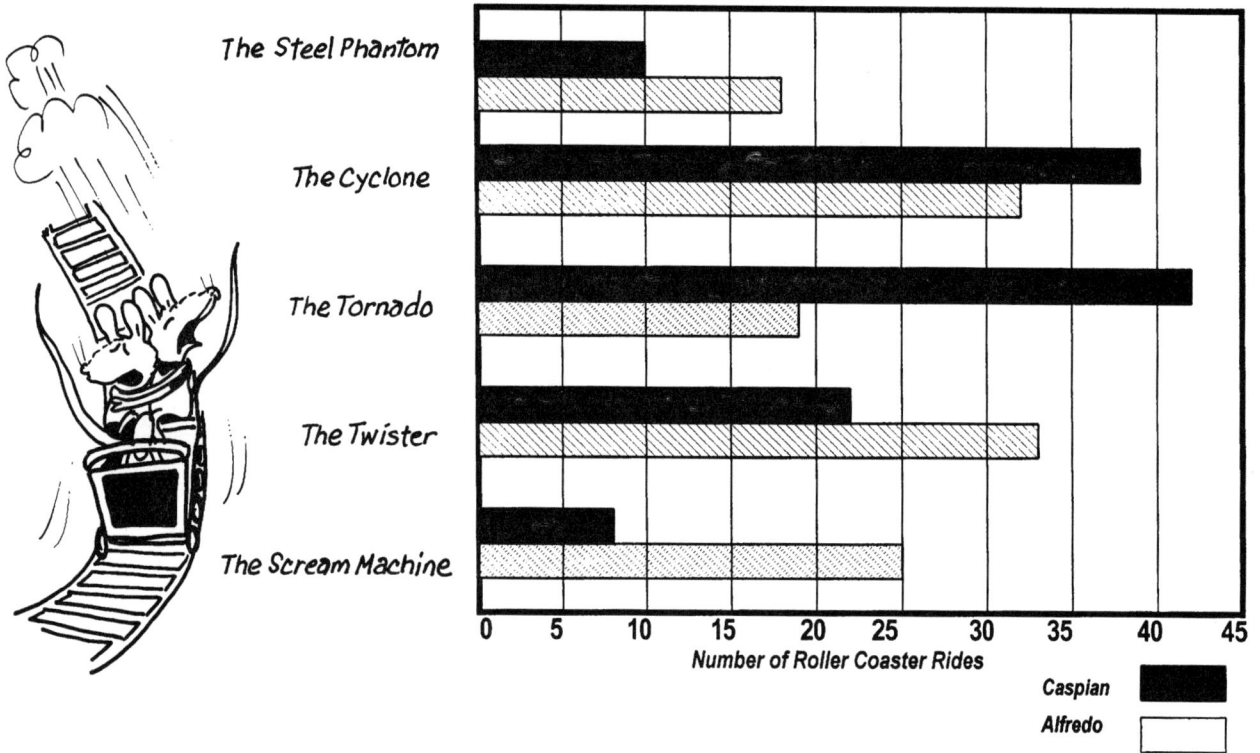

29. About how many times did Caspian ride the Scream Machine? _____

30. How many more times did Alfredo ride the Steel Phantom than Caspian? _____

31. Who rode a coaster about 38 times? _____

    Which coaster? _____

32. Which coaster did one rider ride 25 times more than the other rider?

    _____

33. Which coasters were ridden about 18 times by the same rider? _____

    _____

34. Who rode The Twister 22 times?

    _____

35. Which coaster was ridden about 8 times by Caspian?

    _____

Name _____

Fourth Grade Book of Math Tests   Copyright ©2000 by Incentive Publications, Inc., Nashville, TN.

KEEPING TRACK OF SKILLS

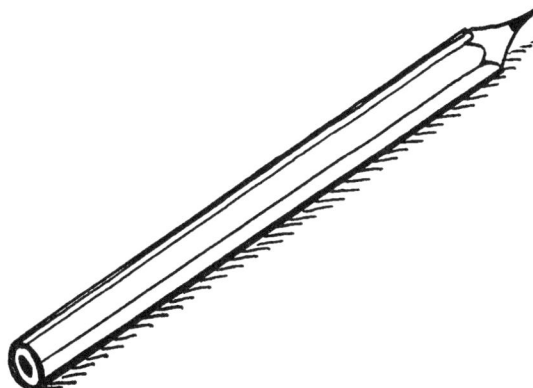

STUDENT PROGRESS RECORD FORM — MATH SKILLS

Student Name _____

TEST DATE	NUMBERS & COMPUTATION TESTS	SCORE	OF	COMMENTS & NEEDS
	Test # 1 Whole Number Concepts	of	45	
	Test # 2 Addition & Subtraction	of	50	
	Test # 3 Multiplication	of	40	
	Test # 4 Division	of	40	
	Test # 5 All Operations	of	30	
	Test # 5 Fractions	of	50	
	Test # 7 Decimals	of	40	
	Test # 8 Algebra Concepts	of	30	

TEST DATE	PROBLEM-SOLVING TESTS	SCORE	OF	COMMENTS & NEEDS
	Test # 1 Approaches to Problems	of	20	
	Test # 2 Problem-Solving Strategies	of	20	
	Test # 3 Problems to Solve, Part 1	of	40	
	Test # 4 Problems to Solve, Part 2	of	30	
	Test # 5 Problem-Solving Process	of	25	

TEST DATE	GEOMETRY & MEASUREMENT TESTS	SCORE	OF	COMMENTS & NEEDS
	Test # 1 Plane Geometry	of	60	
	Test # 2 Space Geometry	of	25	
	Test # 3 Measurement	of	75	

TEST DATE	GRAPHING, STATISTICS, & PROBABILITY TESTS	SCORE	OF	COMMENTS & NEEDS
	Test # 1 Coordinate Graphing	of	55	
	Test # 2 Probability	of	30	
	Test # 3 Statistics	of	30	
	Test # 4 Statistics & Graphs	of	35	

Fourth Grade Book of Math Tests

CLASS PROGRESS RECORD
MATH SKILLS
(Numbers & Computation)

Class _____

Teacher _____

NUMBERS & COMPUTATION TESTS

TEST DATE	TEST	COMMENTS ABOUT RESULTS	SKILLS NEEDING RE-TEACHING
	Test # 1 Whole Number Concepts		
	Test # 2 Addition and Subtraction		
	Test # 3 Multiplication		
	Test # 4 Division		
	Test # 5 All Operations		
	Test # 6 Fractions		
	Test # 7 Decimals		
	Test # 8 Algebra Concepts		

Fourth Grade Book of Math Tests

CLASS PROGRESS RECORD — MATH SKILLS

(Problem Solving, Geometry & Measurement, and Graphing, Statistics, & Probability)

Class _____   Teacher _____

PROBLEM-SOLVING TESTS

TEST DATE	TEST	COMMENTS ABOUT RESULTS	SKILLS NEEDING RE-TEACHING
	Test # 1 Approaches to Problems		
	Test # 2 Problem-Solving Strategies		
	Test # 3 Problems to Solve, Part 1		
	Test # 4 Problems to Solve, Part 2		
	Test # 5 Problem-Solving Process		

GEOMETRY & MEASUREMENT TESTS

TEST DATE	TEST	COMMENTS ABOUT RESULTS	SKILLS NEEDING RE-TEACHING
	Test # 1 Plane Geometry		
	Test # 2 Space Geometry		
	Test # 3 Measurement		

GRAPHING, STATISTICS, & PROBABILITY TESTS

TEST DATE	TEST	COMMENTS ABOUT RESULTS	SKILLS NEEDING RE-TEACHING
	Test # 1 Coordinate Graphing		
	Test # 2 Probability		
	Test # 3 Statistics		
	Test # 4 Statistics & Graphs		

GOOD SKILL SHARPENERS
FOR MATH SKILLS

The tests in this book will identify student needs for practice, re-teaching or reinforcement of basic skills. Once those areas of need are known, some good ways to strengthen those skills must be found.

The BASIC/Not Boring Skills Series, published by Incentive Publications (www.incentivepublications.com), offers 14 books to sharpen basic skills at the Grades 4–5 level. Four of these books are full of math exercises.

The pages of these books are student-friendly, clever, and challenging—guaranteed not to be boring! They cover a wide range of skills, including the skills assessed in this book of tests. A complete checklist of skills is available at the front of each book, complete with a reference list directing you to the precise pages for polishing those skills.

TEST IN THIS BOOK 4th Grade Book of Math Tests	Pages in this Book	You will find pages to sharpen skills in these locations from the BASIC/Not Boring Skills Series, published by Incentive Publications.
Numbers & Computation Test # 1 **Whole Number Concepts**	14–19	Gr. 4–5 Computation & Numbers
Numbers & Computation Test # 2 **Addition & Subtraction**	20–25	Gr. 4–5 Computation & Numbers
Numbers & Computation Test # 3 **Multiplication**	26–29	Gr. 4–5 Computation & Numbers
Numbers & Computation Test # 4 **Division**	30–33	Gr. 4–5 Computation & Numbers
Numbers & Computation Test # 5 **All Operations**	34–37	Gr. 4–5 Computation & Numbers
Numbers & Computation Test # 6 **Fractins**	38–43	Gr. 4–5 Computation & Numbers

Name _____

GOOD SKILL SHARPENERS FOR MATH

TEST IN THIS BOOK 4th Grade Book of Math Tests	Pages in this Book	You will find pages to sharpen skills in these locations from the BASIC/Not Boring Skills Series, published by Incentive Publications.
Numbers & Computation Test # 7 **Decimals**	44–47	Gr. 4–5 Computation & Numbers
Numbers & Computation Test # 8 **Algebra Concepts**	48–51	Gr. 4–5 Computation & Numbers Gr. 4–5 Problem Solving
Problem-Solving Test # 1 **Approaches to Problems**	54–57	Gr. 4–5 Problem Solving
Problem-Solving Test # 2 **Problem-Solving Strategies**	58–61	Gr. 4–5 Problem Solving
Problem-Solving Tests # 3 and #4 **Problems to Solve, Part 1** **Problems to Solve, Part 2**	62–67 68–73	Gr. 4–5 Problem Solving Gr. 4–5 Numbers & Computation Gr. 4–5 Geometry & Measurement Gr. 4–5 Graphing, Statistics, & Probability
Problem-Solving Test # 5 **Problem-Solving Process**	74–77	Gr. 4–5 Problem Solving
Geometry & Measurement Test # 1 **Plane Geometry**	80–87	Gr. 4–5 Geometry & Measurement Gr. 4–5 Problem Solving
Geometry & Measurement Test # 2 **Space Geometry**	88–91	Gr. 4–5 Geometry & Measurement Gr. 4–5 Problem Solving
Geometry & Measurement Test # 3 **Measurement**	92–99	Gr. 4–5 Geometry & Measurement Gr. 4–5 Problem Solving
Graphing, Statistics, & Probability Test # 1 **Coordinate Graphing**	102–107	Gr. 4–5 Graphing, Statistics, & Probability Gr. 4–5 Problem Solving
Graphing, Statistics, & Probability Test # 2 **Probability**	108–111	Gr. 4–5 Graphing, Statistics, & Probability
Graphing, Statistics, & Probability Tests # 3 and # 4 **Statistics & Graphing**	112–115 116–120	Gr. 4–5 Graphing, Statistics, & Probability Gr. 4–5 Problem Solving

Name

SCORING GUIDES & ANSWER KEYS

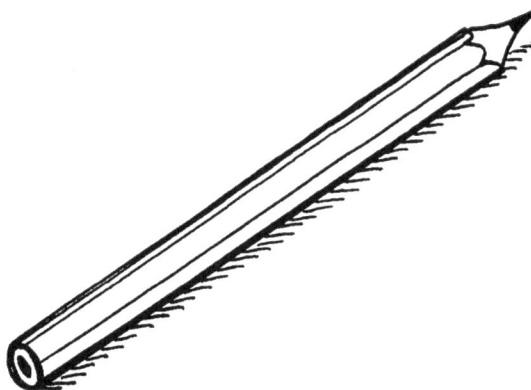

NUMBERS & COMPUTATION TESTS
ANSWER KEY

Whole Number Concepts (Test on page 14)

1. B
2. C
3. six thousand, five hundred, fifty
4. twelve thousand, two hundred
5. 75, 040
6. 125,000
7. 31,100
8. 4,000,000
9. Reggie
10. Georgianna
11. 5,420
12. 101, 110
13. 6,479; 6,505; 6,517
14. A. 5,903
    B. 5,972
    C. 6,430
    D. 6,439
    E. 6,440
    F. 6,493
15. C
16. 7000 + 200 + 40 + 3
17. 8000 + 400 + 90 + 8
18. 2
19. 8
20. hundreds
21. ten thousands
22. Answers may vary. Check to see that there is a 5 in the millions place.
23. 3, 7, 11, 13, 17, 23
24. 3,870
25. 64,200
26. 19,000
27. 20,000
28. number 3 (4000 + 400 + 4)
29. 1, 3, 5, 15
30. 1, 2, 3, 4, 6, 8, 12, 24
31. Cross out: 3, 6, 8, 10, 12
32. Cross out: 4, 8
33. 1, 3, 5, 15
34. 24
35. 21, 39
36. 74 + 47
37. 300, 250, 200
38. Check to see that student has correctly finished the pattern.
39. Hurricanes
40. Speed Kings
41. C
42. A
43. Nellie's
44. Ellie's
45. 151

Fourth Grade Book of Math Tests
Copyright ©2000 by Incentive Publications, Inc., Nashville, TN.

NUMBERS & COMPUTATION TESTS
ANSWER KEY

Addition and Subtraction (Test on page 20)

1–20: The following problems have been answered correctly and should be circled: 1, 2, 3, 6, 7, 9, 13, 14, 15, 17, 18, 19, 20
21. 545
22. 197
23. 926
24. D
25. B
26. 116,063
27. 53
28. 7,600
29. 188
30. yes
31. A and E
32. 117
33. 2,364 seconds
34. 19
35. C
36. 11,093
37. B and C
38. 167
39. A
40. B
41. B and C
42. 37
43. $4075
44. C
45. A
46. A
47. 6
48. 40
49. 250
50. 1001

Multiplication (Test on page 26)

1–20: The following problems have been answered correctly and should be circled: 1, 2, 3, 6, 7, 8, 10, 11, 12, 14, 15, 17, 18, 19, 20
21. 64
22. 150
23. 1176
24. 376,248
25. yes
26. 256
27. 468
28. no
29. 3552
30. A, D, E, and F
31. C
32. 319,708
33. A
34. show: 96605
              96605
         1,062,655
35. 3600
36. 2
37. 6
Answers may vary on 38–40:
38. 5000
39. $12,000
40. 8000

Fourth Grade Book of Math Tests

NUMBERS & COMPUTATION TESTS
ANSWER KEY

Division (Test on page 30)

1–20: The following problems have been answered correctly and should be circled: 3, 5, 6, 7, 10, 11, 12, 13, 14, 15, 16, 17, 18

21. 18
22. t-shirts
23. 23
24. 11,631
25. no
26. 258
27. B
28. 21

29. 3
30. 28 R2
31. A and E
32. 72
33. no
34. 28
35. yes
36. 50
37. 82
38. 50
39. 40
40. 30

All Operations (Test on page 34)

1. D
2. A; 3700 feet
3. B
4. C; 770 miles
5. –
6. ÷
7. ÷
8. ÷
9. +
10. x
11. –
12. B
13. C
14. 96
15. 8000
16. 390

17. 1
18. 1350 ft
19. 900 ft
20. 650 ft
21. 600 ft
22. 6 hours
23. C
24. 82
25. 2
26. 9
27. 54

Answers may vary on 28–30.
28. 400 qt.
29. 9,000
30. 70

Fourth Grade Book of Math Tests

NUMBERS & COMPUTATION TESTS
ANSWER KEY

Fractions (Test on page 38)

1. $\frac{2}{5}$
2. $\frac{3}{5}$
3. $\frac{9}{10}$
4. $\frac{3}{10}$
5. $\frac{1}{5}$
6. $\frac{8}{9}$
7. $\frac{5}{6}$
8. $\frac{2}{3}$
9. $\frac{8}{9}$
10. $6\frac{2}{10}$
11. $21\frac{1}{3}$
12. three fourths
13. seven eighths
14. four ninths
15. four and one third
16. sixteen and three sevenths
17. $\frac{15}{16}$
18. $\frac{1}{16}$
19. $\frac{1}{8}$; $\frac{1}{6}$; $\frac{1}{3}$; $\frac{1}{2}$; $\frac{3}{4}$; $\frac{9}{10}$
20. Gigi
21. Reggie
22. The Comets
23. tonight's game
24. $\frac{2}{3}$; $\frac{2}{5}$; $\frac{5}{6}$; $\frac{3}{7}$
25. $\frac{3}{4}$
26. $\frac{3}{8}$

27. $1\frac{1}{4}$
28. Answers may vary: $\frac{4}{6}$ or $\frac{6}{9}$ or $\frac{8}{12}$ or $\frac{10}{15}$, etc.
29. $\frac{5}{20}$; $\frac{3}{12}$; $\frac{2}{8}$; $\frac{4}{16}$
30. $\frac{3}{4}$
31. $\frac{1}{12}$
32. $\frac{2}{3}$
33. $3\frac{2}{7}$
34. $3\frac{1}{6}$
35. $\frac{9}{2}$
36. $\frac{65}{6}$
37. $\frac{60}{7}$
38. $\frac{2}{9}$
39. $\frac{8}{5}$ or $1\frac{3}{5}$
40. $\frac{4}{6}$ or $\frac{2}{3}$
41. $\frac{11}{40}$
42. no
43. $\frac{3}{24}$ or $\frac{1}{8}$
44. B
45. C
46. $\frac{3}{25}$
47. B
48. 10 years old
49. $\frac{4}{10}$ or $\frac{2}{5}$
50. 23 pairs

Fourth Grade Book of Math Tests

NUMBERS & COMPUTATION TESTS
ANSWER KEY

Decimals (Test on page 44)

1. 0.5
2. 0.05
3. 5.5
4. 5.005
5. 5.05
6. 0.009
7. 9.9
8. 99.9
9. 0.09
10. 900.9
11. 2
12. 0
13. 4
14. 9
15. 7
16. A. Millie
    B. Lilly
    C. Minnie
    D. Ginni
    E. Gigi
    F. Tina
    G. Winnie
17. D
18. 9.1

19. 5.1
20. 100.59
21. C
22. $206.15
23. $841.90
24. J
25. D
26. A
27. E
28. G
29. F
30. B
31. I
32. H
33. A and D
34. B and C
35. 49.3
36. 81.28
37. 55%
38. 36.295
39. 17.25°
40. D

NUMBERS & COMPUTATION TESTS
ANSWER KEY

Algebra Concepts (Test on page 48)

1. −30
   −28
   −21
   −16
   −3
   4
   16
   40

2. equal to

3. less than

4. >

5. <

6. =

7. <

8. >

9. <

10. >

11. B

12. B

13. B

14. A

15. C

16. B

17. D

18. $4 + 3 + n = 15$

19. B

20. 8 hours

21. 0

22. 9

23. 9

24. 45

25. A

26. B or C

27. 10 times

28. C

29. A

30. $350.00

PROBLEM-SOLVING TESTS
ANSWER KEY

Approaches to Problems (Test on page 54)

1–3: Problems 2 and 3 should have X.

4. Cross out:
   15 more of the players were injured during practice.

5. B and D

6. A, B, and C

7. C and D

8. A, B, and E

9. A and C

10. A, B, C, and D

11. the amount of coffee drunk

12. the number of coaches working this year

13. the number of new cheers

14. the number of weeks in the season

15. A

16. D

17. C

18. A and C

19. C

20. B

Problem-Solving Strategies (Test on page 58)

1. D

2. B

3. $1869 \div 3 = n$
   or $1869 \div n = 3$
   or $1869 = 3 \times n$
   or $3 \times n = 1869$
   Answer = 623

4. 31,400 ft.

5. 9 mi

6. 2800 m

7. 2000 ft^2

8. 96 in^3

9. 3 ½

10. 4 + 6

11. Answers may vary.
    Student answer should be about 3000 mi.

12. Answers may vary.
    Student answer should be anywhere from $240 to $250.

13. 1

14. 2:45 pm

15. 350

16. 34

17. 12

18. 207

19. f

20. a

Fourth Grade Book of Math Tests   Copyright ©2000 by Incentive Publications, Inc., Nashville, TN.

PROBLEM-SOLVING TESTS
ANSWER KEY

Problems to Solve, Part 1 (Test on page 62)

1. 13	21. ¾
2. 90	22. 58
3. 4	23. 12.5 mi
4. 139	24. 8.1 min
5. 7 pizzas	25. 28
6. sweatshirt, blanket	26. 9:30 pm
7. no	27. 2:05 pm
8. $22.50	28. 6 hours, 35 minutes
9. $40.90	29. 14 ⅚
10. $12.50	30. ⅜
11. $22.00	31. 9
12. 30	32. 36
13. 19	33. $49.50
14. 66	34. $1305.25
15. 5	35. $87.45
16. 17	36. 6
17. 15	37. $60.25
18. 28	38. $129.00
19. 18	39. $151.05
20. 90	40. $13.00

Fourth Grade Book of Math Tests

PROBLEM-SOLVING TESTS
ANSWER KEY

Problems to Solve, Part 2 (Test on page 68)

1. 125.6 in
2. 12 ft
3. 2920 yd
4. 484,500 yd^2
5. 48 ft^2
6. 12 ft^3
7. 2700 in^3
8. $65
9. $16
10. $257.40
11. 13
12. 39
13. Mol
14. Belva
15. 3
16. Mel

17–21: 18, 19, 20 should be circled.
22. C
23. C
24. B
25. C
26. worm, worm, worm
    worm, minnow, minnow
    minnow, minnow, minnow
    minnow, worm, worm
27. Alfredo and Elmo;
    Alfredo and Reggie;
    Alfredo and Georgio;
    Elmo and Reggie;
    Elmo and Georgio;
    Reggie and Georgio
28. yes
29. no
30. no

Problem-Solving Process (Test on page 74)
Use the scoring guide on page 137 for this test.
Answers to the problems are as follows:

Problem # 1	27.05	Problem # 6	1st – Lou
Problem # 2	32 inches		2nd – Elmo
Problem # 3	72 bars		3rd – Arlo
Problem # 4	8 pieces		4th – Rufus
Problem # 5	168 min, 45 sec OR 2 hours, 48 min, 45 sec	Problem # 7	1$\frac{1}{2}$ hours
		Problem # 8	1:40 A.M.

Fourth Grade Book of Math Tests   Copyright ©2000 by Incentive Publications, Inc., Nashville, TN.

PROBLEM - SOLVING PROCESS SCORING GUIDE

TRAIT	SCORE OF 5	SCORE OF 3	SCORE OF 1
CONCEPTUAL UNDERSTANDING	• Student's work shows that the problem is clearly identified and understood. • Work clearly shows that the student has translated the written problem-solving task effectively into mathematical ideas.	• Student's work shows that the problem is identified and understood. • The student has done an adequate job of translating the written problem-solving task into mathematical ideas.	• Student's work does not show a clear identification or understanding of the problem. • The student has done a partial or incorrect job of translating the written problem-solving task into mathematical ideas.
STRATEGIES & PROCESSES	• Student has chosen appropriate strategies for solving the problem. • The strategies have been used in a complete, clear, and complex manner to move toward a problem solution. • Equations, symbols, models, pictures, and/or diagrams are clear and complete.	• Student has chosen appropriate strategies for solving the problem. • The strategies have been used in a complete, clear, and complex manner to move toward a problem solution. • Equations, symbols, models, pictures, and/or diagrams are complete and relatively clear.	• Student has not chosen appropriate strategies for solving the problem or has chosen appropriate strategies but not used them correctly or effectively. • Equations, symbols, models, pictures and/or diagrams are incomplete or do not lead to the solution.
COMMUNICATION	• The student has used words, symbols, pictures, models, and/or other graphics to clearly show the steps to a solution of the problem. • The student's explanation of the use of strategies and of the path taken to solution is clear and sensible.	• The student has used words, symbols, pictures, models, and/or other graphics to adequately show the steps to a solution of the problem. • The student's explanation of the use of strategies and of the path taken to solution is adequate.	• The student has not adequately used words, symbols, pictures, models, and/or other graphics to clearly show the steps to a solution of the problem. • The communication of the student's processes is skimpy, or nonexistent.
CORRECTNESS (Accuracy of the Answer)	• The student's answer is correct. • The student's work supports the answer given.	• The student's answer is mostly correct, with only minor errors. • The student's work supports the answer.	• The student's answer is incomplete, or incorrect. *and/or* • The student's work does not support the answer given.
VERIFICATION	• The student's work shows that he/she has reviewed the problem-solving process and made a clear, effective attempt to justify the answer or arrive at it in a different way. • The review supports the student's solution.	• The student's work shows that he/she has reviewed the problem-solving process and made an attempt to justify the answer. • The review supports the student's solution.	• The student's work does not show an effective or complete review of his/her process, or a defense or support of his/her solution.

A score of 4 may be given for papers that fall between 3 and 5 on a trait. A score of 2 may be given for papers that fall between 1 and 3.

Fourth Grade Book of Math Tests Copyright ©2000 by Incentive Publications, Inc., Nashville, TN.

GEOMETRY & MEASUREMENT TESTS
ANSWER KEY

Plane Geometry (Test on page 80)

1. D
2. A
3. F
4. C
5. B
6. E
7. C, E, H, and I
8. G and J
9. D
10. A, C, F, and I
11. C, D, and I
12. AB
13. AC, BC, or CD
14. B
15. DG or GD
16. Answers may vary:
    ACH, ADG, BCK, GDE, GJF
17. D
18. A
19. B, C
20. circle
21. 31.4 ft
22. square
23. 16 cm
24. 16 cm^2
25. hexagon
26. 54 in
27. trapezoid
28. 30 ft
29. triangle
30. 38 yd
31. 65 yd^2
32. parallelogram
33. 280 in
34. rectangle
35. 200 m
36. 160 m^2
37. D
38. C
39. B
40. A
41. C
42. B
43. T
44. F
45. T
46. T
47. A, B, E, F, H, I
48. A-E, B-F, C-G, D-H
49. A-J, B-G, C-I, D-H, E-F
50. flip
51. slide
52. turn
53–54. Check to see that student has
       drawn figure accurately.
55. B
56. 314 ft^2
57. C
58. 4500 yd^2
59. 8200 ft^2
60. $4100.00

Fourth Grade Book of Math Tests　　　　Copyright ©2000 by Incentive Publications, Inc., Nashville, TN.

GEOMETRY & MEASUREMENT TESTS
ANSWER KEY

Space Geometry (Test on page 88)

1. rectangular prism
2. sphere
3. cone
4. hexagonal prism
5. cube
6. triangular prism
7. cylinder
8. pyramid
9. hexagonal prism
10. cylinder
11. 6
12. 0
13. cone
14. square or rectangle
15. triangular prism
16. 6
17. 2
18. 9
19. 11
20. 9
21. C
22. B
23. A
24. D
25. # 1

Fourth Grade Book of Math Tests   Copyright ©2000 by Incentive Publications, Inc., Nashville, TN.

GEOMETRY & MEASUREMENT TESTS
ANSWER KEY

Measurement (Test on page 92)

1. weight	28. A	55. 72
2. length	29. C	56. 365 (or 366 for a leap year)
3. capacity	30. D	
4. length	31. C	57. 2:20
5. length	32. B	58. 7:00
6. length	33. A	59. A
7. length	34. A	60. B
8. weight	35. C	61. B
9. time	36. <	62. A
10. capacity	37. <	63. Answers may vary. Check to see that student answers are accurate.
11. length	38. >	
12. weight	39. <	
13. capacity	40. <	
14. length	41. >	
15. temperature	42. =	64. 138 ft
16. time	43. >	65. 37.68 ft
17. B	44. =	66. 18 ft^2
18. E	45. >	67. 314 ft^2
19. C	46. 360	68. 3400 ft
20. D	47. 1	69. 6000 yd^2
21. B	48. 30	70. 7000 ft^2
22. D	49. 180	71. 4096 ft^3
23. A	50. 10	72. D
24. D	51. 1	73. C
25. B	52. 12	74. 3 mi
26. D	53. 63	75. 40 ft
27. D	54. 96	

GRAPHING, STATISTICS, & PROBABILITY TESTS ANSWER KEY

Coordinate Graphing (Test on page 102)

1–4: Descriptions of shoes may vary. Students may draw shoes, also.

1. baby shoe or slipper

2. basketball shoe or gym shoe or tennis shoe

3. high top gym shoe or basketball shoe or gym shoe

4. boot

5. (4, 3)

6. (1, 9)

7. (2, 2)

8. (5, 6)

9. (6, 8)

10. (3, 5)

11. (3, 7)

12. (6, 1)

13. (14, 8)

14. (11, 1); (2, 8); (2, 1); (4, 4); (9, 7)

15–22. Check to see that student has drawn worms in the correct places.

23. N

24. U

25. M

26. O

27. P

28. (–4, 9); (–3, 9); (0, 2)

29. (4, 5)

30. (–1, 10)

31. (2, 3)

32. (4, 2); (–5, 6); (–3, 6)

33–42. Check to see that student has drawn items in the correct places.

43. swim fin

44. volleyball or ball of any sort

45. goggles

46. football

47. bowling ball

48. skateboard

49. (–6, –3)

50. (2, 6)

51. (0, –6)

52. (–5, –2)

53. (–5, 4)

54. (7, 4)

55. If students plot points and draw accurately, the figure will be a sailboat.

Fourth Grade Book of Math Tests

GRAPHING, STATISTICS, & PROBABILITY TESTS ANSWER KEY

Probability (Test on page 108)

1. C
2. B
3. D
4. B
5. H,H; T,T; H,T; (may add a 4th option of T, H)
6. 5
7. caramel-tuna
8. onion
9. broccoli and pizza-lime
10. A
11. 1/4
12. 3/4
13. Gracie and Ellie; Gracie and Abby; Gracie and Millie; Ellie and Abby, Ellie and Millie; Millie and Abby
14. 2/20 or 1/10
15. 6/20 or 3/10
16. 12/20 or 6/10 or 2/5
17. 14/20 or 7/10
18. 4/9
19. 3/9 or 1/3
20. 7/9
21. 14/18 or 7/9
22. 7/18
23. 5/18
24. 12/18 or 2/3 or 6/9
25. 4/12 or 1/3
26. 2/12 or 1/6
27. 6/12 or 1/2
28. 6/12 or 1/2
29. 2/12 or 1/6
30. elephant

Statistics (Test on page 112)

1. D
2. F
3. B
4. A
5. H
6. I
7. 10
8. 8–12
9. 11–15
10. 21
11. 28
12. 16–30
13. 14
14. adults
15. Saturday
16. 3
17. chocolate pie
18. 58 inches
19. 47 feet
20. 44 feet
21. cooked eggs
22. 1 minute, 10 seconds
23. raw eggs
24. spaghetti and cooked eggs
25. peach pits
26. Vinnie
27. 39 feet
28. 16 feet
29. 30 feet–46 feet
30. yes; Minnie and Vinnie

Fourth Grade Book of Math Tests   Copyright ©2000 by Incentive Publications, Inc., Nashville, TN.

GRAPHING, STATISTICS, & PROBABILITY TESTS ANSWER KEY

Statistics & Graphs (Test on page 116)

1. 4
2. Rufus
3. Waldo
4. Mimi
5. about 33
6. Rufus
7. Week 7
8. 13 inches
9. 2, 3, 6
10. 8 and 9
11. $25
12. $47
13. $4
14. $100
15. 45
16. Angie
17. 3
18. Georgia
19. Winnie
20. Millie
21. 35
22. July
23. 10
24. Caspian's
25. Rufus
26. no
27. December
28. July and August
29. approx. 8
30. approx. 8
31. Caspian, The Cyclone
32. The Tornado
33. The Steel Phantom and The Tornado
34. Caspian
35. The Scream Machine

Fourth Grade Book of Math Tests   Copyright ©2000 by Incentive Publications, Inc., Nashville, TN.